"What an incredible and timely r[...] Holmes. *Redefined* beautifully con[...] Beatitudes and practical life application. Allen shares some of his own life stories and how important it is for all of us to have the correct view of what a genuine relationship with God really is. A relationship with Jesus is so much more than checking "to do" boxes. *Redefined* is a must-read for every person wanting to Re-ignite and Re-vision your life in a way you have never fully experienced."

—LEE DOMINGUE
Author of Pearls of the King and The Family Meeting Guide
Founder of Kingdom Builders U.S., Legacy Pastor of Church of the
Highlands, Birmingham, Alabama

"The genius of Allen Holmes' book, *Redefined*, is that he is able, through this writing, to make deep truths accessible. You get it! He writes in such a way as to make it simple. But he doesn't dumb it down. He makes it livable. Life-changing!"

—MICHAEL FLETCHER,
Senior Pastor, Manna Church

"The world needs more life-giving churches! Churches that teach people how to walk with Jesus so that we can change our world. If you are looking for a book that will help you understand what it means to follow Jesus and experience a blessed life, this book is for you!"

—GREG SURRATT
ARC President and Founding Pastor of Seacoast Church in Mt. Pleasant, SC.

"What I love most about Allen Holmes is how he loves hurting people. I have witnessed time and time again Allen come alongside a beat up, tired, or burned out pastor to be a friend. He has a direct, but gracious way of leading people into a deeper relationship with Jesus so they can experience redemption through their crisis. If you are tired of religion, if you are hurting, if you have drifted away from Jesus this book will breathe new life into your soul!"

—DINO RIZZO

Executive Director of ARC (Association of Related Churches) and Associate Pastor at Church of the Highlands, Birmingham, AL

"America is full of hurting, discouraged people. Jesus stepped into a similar context and said, 'come to me all who are weary and carry heavy burdens.' Every time Allen visits our church, I hear Jesus inviting the weary to draw near and find rest. If you are hurting, discouraged or know someone who is, read this book. Jesus is inviting you to draw near, to rest, to be blessed!"

—MATTHEW BARNETT

Founder of the LA Dream Center and Senior Pastor of Angelus Temple.

FOREWORD BY CHRIS HODGES

Pastor, Church of the Highlands

redefined*

re·de·fined | /ˌrēdəˈfīned/

*A SIMPLE PATH TO
A HOPE-FILLED LIFE

DR. ALLEN HOLMES

With Jesse Barnett

Published by Definition Press

ISBN: 978-1-7377626-0-7 (Paperback)
ISBN: 978-1-7377626-1-4 (Kindle)
First edition.

DEDICATION

To my mentor Dr. Bill Bennett. Dr. Bennett and I met in 1997 when my life was falling apart. Dr. Bennett was 74, a retired pastor and a friend of pastors. He spent the last 20 years of his life mentoring and fathering me. When we were together in public, he would introduce me as his son. It was Dr. Bennett, in the middle of my crisis, who taught me how to be with Jesus which transformed my life. For years, Dr. Bennett urged me to begin writing. He would say, "anything worth saying is worth writing." I know he would love this book. Dr. Bennett, I miss your love, friendship, encouragement, and corny jokes. Your life had such a profound impact on my life and I cannot wait to see you again!

There are several other people I want to thank:

Tina, thank you for being patient with me. Life-change takes time and your beauty, grace, and friendship have been such an inspiration to me. You are my favorite person in the whole world and I am so lucky to be your husband.

Definition Church, thank you for allowing me to be your pastor. I love our church family. My family and I have been so blessed by this community. Despite my imperfection, for the last 20 years, you have trusted me to help you become all that God wants you to be. The best is yet to come!

Jesse Barnett, thank you for all your hard work on this book. I had no idea this first book would go so well and the truth is it would not have without your help.

Civil Creative and *Sam Tesh,* thank you for believing in me and Definition Church. You helped us rebrand and helped me take a bold step into a new season of ministry and I am so grateful.

TABLE OF CONTENTS

FOREWORD

W hen our kids were growing up, my wife and I noticed that as each one entered adolescence, they began to redefine themselves. Seemingly overnight, our daughter, Sarah, went from being a little girl playing with stuffed animals to a young woman experimenting with nail polish and lipstick. With our four sons, each one chose to mark his entrance into young adulthood with a radically different haircut than the "little boy" style he'd been wearing. For both genders, this adolescent redefining process also included buying new jeans and shoes that always seemed to cost more than the last pair.

While I didn't always agree with their fashion choices, I understood their desire to express themselves in a more adult, or at least peer-approved, manner. The funny thing, though, is that despite whatever fads and fashions they tried, each child remained uniquely and distinctly who they are and had always been. Because ultimately, redefining who they are became a matter of which sources they consulted.

On one hand, they could be influenced by their friends, classmates, social media heroes and followers, along with the messages from online media, TV, and movies. When these proved insubstantial, however, they could come back to what we had taught them is the ultimate source of their identity, God's Word. Relying on Scripture and their relationship with God, maturity then became a journey of discovery as they explored *how* God made them, *why* He made them, and *what* He created them specifically to do in this life. Basically, they learned that the real discovery of redefining themselves takes place on the inside.

I suspect this redefining-as-maturing process is one we all experience, regardless of our age, when we first encounter God and invite Jesus into our heart. From there, our spiritual journey is often a matter of seeking, finding, failing, forgiving, and persevering. No matter how much we may try to grow closer to God in a sequential, step-by-step, chronological process, our reality is usually messier. We take one leap forward and two steps back. We obey and focus on our relationship with the Lord until we're pulled away by various urgent demands or alluring temptations.

Along the way and throughout our process, we discover new facets of God's character, new dimensions to His love, and more relevant truths in His Word. We also learn more about who we are. We realize we don't know as much as we once thought we did. Humbled and teachable again, we revisit certain aspects of what we believe and why we believe them. We begin to grasp a new understanding of what it means to be spiritually mature as we redefine our faith by going deeper in our relationship with God. Otherwise, we remain stagnant—stuck in our immaturity.

In fact, the author of Hebrews, writing to the followers of Jesus at Corinth, warned them about falling away from their faith and instructed them to reconsider their spiritual nourishment.

"You need milk, not solid food!" he wrote. "Anyone who lives on milk, being still an infant, is not acquainted with the teaching about righteousness. But solid food is for the mature, who by constant use have trained themselves to distinguish good from evil" (Hebrews 5:12-14, NIV).

The author of this book you're holding, Allen Holmes, knows this same truth, that when we're in danger of falling away, sliding back, and giving up we must redefine our faith. And I can't think of anyone better qualified than Allen to infuse our current understanding of being a Christian with a fresh perspective. I'm biased, of course, because I've known Allen for more than a decade now, ever since he introduced himself at one of our first GROW conferences. From his friendly demeanor to his thoughtful questions, he radiated a passion for knowing God and sharing His love with the world around us in a deeply personal way.

As we got better acquainted, Allen asked me to mentor him, a privilege I agreed to take on. It's humbling to pastor another pastor, and I made it clear to Allen that I didn't have all the answers, but that I know the One who does. Over the years I've been blessed to watch Allen grow and mature in his faith. While we communicate almost every month, I've especially enjoyed the in-person visits two or three times a year when we can spend time learning, growing, and fellowshipping together. We have both discovered more of what it means to follow the example of Christ, leading others by serving them.

One of the most dramatic ways Jesus served others was to redefine their understanding of faith, religion, and grace. And that's what this book is all about. Drawing on the first public sermon Jesus gave, the Sermon on the Mount, and His opening blessings, the Beatitudes, Allen explores just how shocking Christ's new definitions must have been for his listeners. They were accustomed to the rigors of the Jewish religion, a culturally complex system that relied on merit and a hierarchy more social than spiritual. There was no room for grace.

Then suddenly Jesus, this carpenter's son from Nazareth, showed up and turned their notions upside down. Instead of reinforcing a religious system, the Messiah invited his listeners to experience a relationship with the Living God, a merciful Father who loved them enough to send His only Son to forgive their sins. Jesus made it clear it's not about outward appearances and pleasing Jewish leaders but about what's in our hearts. It's about divine relationship, not human religion.

Consequently, Christ forever redefined how we know God.

Redefined literally means to define something again. But the very necessity of defining something more than once is revealing in itself: either the concept being redefined has been misunderstood, its meaning has changed contextually, previous definitions were lacking, or all the above. As followers of Jesus, we discover redefining our understanding of faith is essential to our spiritual maturity.

Which is why I'm so excited about this book. With his careful exploration of the Beatitudes and the Sermon on the Mount, Allen takes us back to Jesus' initial redefinition of what faith is all about. The result is a breath of fresh air that will cut through the social, cultural, and religious clutter that may be distracting you from knowing God and following Jesus. Whether you're unsure what it means to be an authentic Christian in our 21st century world or you're tired of people misunderstanding your relationship with the Lord, Redefined is for you.

Don't get stuck. Don't get distracted. Don't settle for milk.

Don't cling to what others have conditioned you to believe about God when He invites you to experience knowing Him for yourself. If you want to mature in your faith and discover more of your true identity in Christ, then enjoy the solid food of God's Word that's about to be served in these pages!

—CHRIS HODGES

Pastor, Church of the Highlands

Author of What's Next? and Out of the Cave

Introduction

A Life Undefined

It was a night I can never forget, although looking back, twenty-four years later, I shouldn't be surprised—no one can forget when the only world they've known comes crashing down around them.

It burns into your memory and shapes the rest of your life.

If you think of your life like the scenes in a movie, that one would have had all the elements of the climax in a drama.

After ten years of marriage, my dad was done.

He picked up his suitcase, turned, and walked out of the front door and out of our lives.

He never came back.

We lived in a small house in Wilmington, North Carolina. I was five years old, and my baby sister was just two. Mom and I were sitting side-by-side on our small second-hand couch; my sister played on the floor.

With two small kids to raise as a now single mother, my mom knew that her high school diploma wasn't enough. So after a period of grieving, she went back to school. In between working at least two jobs at once, she squeezed in her classes, housework, and taking care of her kids.

With my dad out of the picture and Mom working so hard to provide for us, it left me with a lot of free time on my hands. This taught me a powerful lesson that embedded itself in my mind at a very early age—*I was on my own, and if it was going to happen, it was up to me.* This spirit of independence and self-sufficiency served me well for years but would eventually almost destroy my life.

When I reflect on my childhood, it seems good, and it seems normal. Kids are resilient, and this new normal was all I knew, so at first, I was happy. With that spirit of independence and self-sufficiency, I started working in fifth grade delivering the paper and cutting grass around the neighborhood.

My mom eventually remarried, but neither my biological father nor my stepfather was very involved in my life. My dad had moved to a town four hours away, so I did not see him often; my stepfather lived just down the hall but worked all the time. A college professor, he also headed up the literacy council and ran the local food bank. Ironically, while he was working hard to save the world, I was falling apart in his home. He did not have time and did not seem interested in me—my sports, academics, or church activities—and this created a lot of tension in our relationship. He had very high expectations for me but was completely unengaged with my life. He barked out plenty of orders but never expressed any love or approval. In fact, the only thing he would express to me was his disappointment.

Once again, I was on my own and not sure if I would ever measure up.

By the weeks leading up to my eighth-grade year, the situation at home had deteriorated almost beyond repair. My stepfather and I were always fighting; I was constantly in trouble at school, and my grades were awful. He and my mom were desperate. They were not sure what to do with me, but it was obvious the path I was on was not headed in a good direction. We met with the school guidance counselor and concluded that if I was not able to turn things around, they would be forced to send me to a boarding school.

The school year began, and as an eighth-grader, I was eligible to play football. One day, after getting into trouble in class (again), I had two brief but life-changing conversations. The first was with my vice-principal. He told me he thought I had real potential as a football player. In fact, he even thought I could play college football one day. However, he said that in order to do that I needed to do my best in the classroom.

Since we were on a first-name basis, this clearly wasn't happening.

In what may have been a calculated one-two punch, my football coach also pulled me aside after practice. He told me he wanted me on the team but he was getting bad reports from my teachers. In that gruff way that only coaches have, he put his arm around my shoulders, gave me a hard squeeze, and said, "Son, if you want to remain on *my* team, you need to get your act together in the classroom."

For whatever reason, those two conversations were *exactly* what I needed to hear, and their words stuck. I decided to make some changes to the way I was handling myself. First, I started applying myself in school. From that day on, I never got in trouble again at school, and I never made less than a B in any class. (Until I got to seminary. Seminary was hard!) Second, I decided to start attending church. Church was great for me. I made new friends, was loved and encouraged by several families, really connected with my youth pastor, and began to discover my passion for ministry. Third, I started playing sports all year long. I played football, basketball, and baseball. This constant activity kept me out of trouble, provided lots of friends, and taught me valuable life lessons.

Through all this I discovered something about myself—if I worked hard, I could be successful in school, at church, and in sports. Finally, I was winning, and it felt great! For the next several years I appeared to have it all together. As I moved into high school, I was excelling at school, sports, and church. Everyone was amazed by my turnaround.

Life was good, and I loved all the attention my performance gained me.

I graduated and headed off to college at the University of North Carolina at Wilmington, where I realized God was calling me into vocational ministry. I was very involved serving in church, and ministry became my greatest passion. I finished my undergraduate degree at UNCW, married Tina, my college sweetheart, and was off to seminary.

I was living the dream!

Seminary was like heaven on earth. I was surrounded by men and women who loved Jesus. Every day I was being taught the Bible by some of the world's greatest theologians and America's best pastors. I was making new friends who wanted to change the world, and I was married to the woman of my dreams.

But suddenly, and unexpectedly, everything came crashing down.

In early April, with the spring semester winding down, I came home after class to find Tina lying in bed and crying. We were still newlyweds; we'd only been married for five months. Tina's move to Wake Forest and her transition to married life had been more difficult for her than it was for me. She had grown up in a very close family and had left behind lifelong friends. I, on the other hand, grew up in a broken family and had moved eighteen times before getting married. Home was a moving target.

She was working a full-time job for the first time as an assistant manager in retail. I was in school full-time *and* working 25 hours a week at night and on the weekends, just like I did all through college. This life and schedule felt great to me but overwhelming to Tina. I would leave in the morning for class before she got up. She would then go to work all day and on her way home I would pass her as I made my way to work. We were in a new city, at a new church, and trying to make new friends.

We were both working very hard and did not have time to invest in our new marriage. We were away from both family and friends. Again, this seemed normal to me. It was how I grew up. Independent, self-reliant, and hard working. Give me a challenge, and I was all in for the climb. For Tina, this was all physically, emotionally, and relationally overwhelming. She was falling apart, and as a young husband, I didn't see the signs. Even if I did, I really didn't know how to help.

Finally, Tina reached her breaking point.

As we talked that afternoon, Tina said to me through her tears, "I don't love you. I don't think I want to be married; I will never be in the ministry, and I am moving back home." At that moment, everything that was important to me began slipping through my hands. I was losing my marriage and my dream of being in ministry.

How could this happen? The answer to that question is what this book is all about!

That afternoon changed my life.

Tina didn't leave, but because of her honesty that day, over the next few years, we learned many things about life and marriage. The most important lesson was this—*I did not know how to cultivate or maintain a personal relationship with God, with Tina, or with anyone else.*

The pressure we were under and the changes we experienced exposed the weakness in all my relationships. From the outside, I looked like I had it all together, but underneath, the foundation was rotted and weak.

Theologically, I was "saved". Like a lot of Christians, I had trusted Jesus for forgiveness and salvation, but I had no idea how to *talk* to Him, *listen* to Him, *follow* Him, or allow Him to transform my life.

Legally, I was "married", but I had no idea how to connect with my wife *spiritually* or *emotionally*. Previously, she'd had rich connections from family and friends; now we were alone, and the issues in our relationship came bubbling up to the surface.

I was working *for* God and Tina but did not understand how to allow God's Spirit to work *in* me. That independence and self-reliance I'd spent years honing to a razor-sharp edge were destroying me. I wanted to earn God's approval but did not understand approval was not something I could earn. God's approval comes by faith in the redemptive work of Christ. I was living under the law but was desperate to learn how to live under grace.

I couldn't see it yet, but everything I knew about faith was wrong.

And if I couldn't redefine this foundation, I was in trouble.

A Blessed Life

In John 15, Jesus teaches the well-known parable of the vine and the branches. Using the metaphor of a vine, fruit, and a gardener, he explains to his disciples the key to life was for them to remain connected to the vine.

Of course, the vine represents the connection to God through His son Jesus.

Stay connected, and we will live fruitful lives.

Disconnect, and you are cast aside and worthless.

I did not know how to have that kind of relationship with Christ. I did not know how to have that kind of relationship with Tina. In fact, I did not understand relationships at all. All of my life I believed I was on my own and success was up to me. I was independent, self-sufficient, and driven—and I liked it that way. I was *desperately* trying to win the approval of my new wife, my friends, my professors, my parents, and ultimately God.

My relationships were all *unintentionally conditional* because I didn't feel I could ever measure up. I was religious—which meant all work, no relationship. I was working hard; that's something I knew how to do well. But it was work in my own strength; it was *for* God but independently *of* him, and it was exhausting.

For years, I had been a success wherever I'd put my effort. People admired me and wanted to be like me. I was good at everything. Even all my friends' parents wanted them to be more like me.

Augustine said, "Pray as though everything depends on God, but work as if everything depends on you." I had the second part down to a science, so I was proud of my performance, my discipline, my obedience, and my zeal. But it was almost all *me*, and no *God*.

Suddenly, through the tears of my heartbroken and overwhelmed wife, I could see that all my hard work wasn't enough. Not even close. I was exposed. My marriage crisis humbled me, broke me, and brought me to a place of surrender and dependence.

But through it all, something amazing happened—it empowered me to love my wife. It was strange. When my family and friends thought I should be mad at Tina for saying she wanted to leave me, I discovered a love for her that surprised me. I did not understand what was happening. How could I feel so much love, mercy, and desire for someone who was rejecting me?

I was not *trying* to love her; I simply could not help it.

Something was happening inside me that I could not explain.

I knew that if I had any hope of becoming the husband, the pastor, and the man I wanted to be in this life, then I had to figure some things out before moving forward.

As we dropped out of seminary and moved back home to try to rebuild our marriage, I had this strange, inexplicable faith that God was doing something in that moment that would change everything. For the first time in my life, I was free from the burden of performance and managing everyone's expectations. I didn't quite understand it at the time, but I was getting a taste of the life we were all created for. In the midst of my crisis, which was the most painful moment of my life, I began to discover a new life, a *blessed* life.

A lot of people use that term loosely to mean a variety of things. Most of them have to do with more or better *stuff*. But in the midst of this storm, I discovered what blessed truly means. In Matthew 11:28 Jesus said, "Come to me, all of you who are weary and carry heavy burdens, and I will give you rest. Take my yoke upon you. Let me teach you, because I am humble and gentle at heart, and you will find rest for your souls. For my yoke is easy to bear and the burden I give you is light."

This is the Christian life! It is a life of humble dependence. It is not working *for* Him but *with* Him. I read this verse with new eyes, and it changed me from the independent and self-reliant achiever I'd always been, to a wholly-dependent and helpless-without-God servant.

Here's the lesson we don't always want to learn: once we come to the end of ourselves and turn to Jesus in desperation, we discover *new life*. When we are "yoked" to Jesus, He does the heavy lifting, and we find rest. We can lay down the burdens of religion, self-sufficiency, independence, and performance, and trust in the work of Christ for us and in us.

We begin to focus on being rather than doing.

We begin to feel his love and acceptance.

We begin to appreciate the beauty of the Gospel.

We begin to experience joy.

We begin to fall in love with Jesus.

We begin to live from our heart, which is captivated by the grace and generosity of God. He begins producing His life in us. This is the Christian life. This is what Jesus came to accomplish. This is the blessed life!

Life Undefined

My story is basically the American story in a nutshell. We are religious, and we want to do good, but somewhere between our heads and our hearts, we have lost God. We pride ourselves on our independence. We are "self-made." We are far more concerned about *what* we do than *who* we are. We have lots of acquaintances but very few friends. We know all *about* God but do not know how to develop our relationship into a friendship with Him. We want Jesus to get us to heaven, but we are unsure of how he can help us with our family, our work, or the heartbreaking issues in our world. We believe God has a big set of rules that we doubt we can never live up to, but we do not understand His love for us, His desire to commune with us, and His willingness to carry our burdens.

It's a fuzzy faith with poorly-defined edges and uncertain application.

This is a problem, not only in our relationship with God, but also in our relationships with each other. Our relationships have been distilled down to simple transactions. What do you want from me, and what should I expect from you? This kind of thinking produces a relational tug-of-war with our spouse, our kids, our friends, our co-workers, and our neighbors. The problem with a relational tug-of-war is someone always finds themselves with blisters on their hands and covered in mud.

Why has this become such a problem?

Honestly, I am not sure I am the best person to answer that question. I am certainly not a sociologist, but after more than 20 years in ministry, seeing people at their very best and very worst, I do have a few thoughts.

First, we all long to live a blessed life. Most people in the world would not use that language, but the desire for blessing indwells us all. Mankind was created for Eden, and we've been trying to find our way back there whether we realize that or not. We want to be happy but fail to understand that our happiness, the very blessed life we were created for and searching for, is *dependent* upon a healthy and growing relationship with God.

Most people seek happiness independently of God and wonder why nothing fills the void. In fact, this is a pretty good stripped-down description of our sinful nature. We are created in God's image, but sin separates us from relationship.

Sin is our declaration of independence, and it is killing us.

Sadly, this is how our story began.

In the Garden of Eden, "God created the heavens and earth." All that God created was good (Genesis 1:31). The sacred beauty and majesty of Heaven touched the water, dirt, and sky of earth. God and man walked in the coolness of the garden—together.

Life was good.

God's plan in the very beginning was to create mankind in His image, to rule and reign with Him, under His authority, for His glory and the blessing of all people. God wanted to share Himself with us. He created us for relationship with Him and each other, and all that we needed for life would flow out of that relationship.

In Genesis 2:15, God commissioned Adam to "tend and watch over" the garden. My Hebrew professor, John Sailhamer, who is the editor of Genesis in the Expositor's Commentary and the author of *The Pentateuch as Narrative*, as well as several other books on the Old Testament and Hebrew Language, says this translation is the result of a scribal error. He argues quite convincingly that this verse should be translated, "The Lord placed the man in the Garden of Eden to **worship and obey.**"

This translation is supported by a close examination of the original language, fits the narrative of the story, and coincides with the overall message of the scripture. The idea here is that God put Adam and Eve in the garden to enjoy Him and to enjoy each other. He did not create them to work. Work was the result of the fall (Genesis 3:17-19). He did have work for them to do, but God would provide all they needed as they walked with Him, and they ruled together over all of creation. Everything they needed for life, for relationships, and to rule would flow out of their relationship with God.

However, in Genesis 3, Satan convinces Adam and Eve that God is holding out on them. Satan convinces them that they can have it all, without God, independent of His oppression. What Adam and Eve failed to understand, and what we still misunderstand today, is that *they already had it all, and God was doing the heavy lifting.* They were created to rule, to be a King and Queen, and build a royal family in paradise.

The world was perfect. No sin, no hard labor, no sickness, pain, disease, or death. No storms, no earthquakes, no plagues. No corruption, no abuse, and no slavery. However, Satan convinced them, if they declared their independence, they could be like God.

Their ambition and desire for independence blinded them to the fact that *they were already like God.* They were created in His image to rule and reign with Him (Genesis 1:27), to reflect His glory and enjoy His creation, but they were deceived. They decided to play God. They wanted to decide for themselves what was right and wrong. They did not want God or anyone else ruling over them.

In a moment that would change the world, they ate, and everything changed.

Heaven and earth were ripped apart.

God and man were separated by sin.

Adam and Eve introduced evil, pain, suffering, rebellion, independence, pride, war, and death into God's good creation. When the intimate, lifegiving connection between God and man was severed, all of creation suffered—including you and me. Adam and Eve sinned first, but our relationship with God has suffered ever since. Rather than enjoying and receiving from God, we began to hide. Rather than walking with unabashed intimacy, we began to cover ourselves in shame. We create a public image to hide our private sin. We are full of guilt, shame, and fear.

Not only did our relationship with God suffer, but our relationships with each other were affected as well. We became victims, pointing fingers, and placing blame. Control and power struggles replaced love. We fight for our rights rather than fighting for our relationships.

All of creation suffered as a result of one choice. Paradise was lost, and our perfect home of safety, beauty, abundance, and delight began to die. We were put out of the garden and forced to work, to suffer under the sun, and to carry the burden of provision (Genesis 3:17-24).

Since that day, we have had one overwhelming desire—to get back to Eden. C.S. Lewis once said, "If I find in myself desires which nothing in this world can satisfy, the only logical explanation is that I was made for another world." We were made for another world; we can all feel it. Most do not understand the origin or object of their desire, but it all goes back to the garden where paradise was lost.

The question is, how do we get back there?

How do we find our way home?

How do we redefine what it means to live a life of faith?

In this twisted world where things seem to be spiraling out of control, where is Eden?

We have been reaching for heaven ever since the fall, but no matter how high we climb, no matter what we achieve, no matter how much we learn, we are still a long way from home. We experience glimpses of paradise. We get a taste of heaven in the ecstasy of love, in the beauty of creation, the satisfaction of food, in the complexity of the universe, in the birth of a new baby, or the wrinkled face of a beloved and wise elder. Each of these delights only increases our appetite, our longing for home.

Many have tried to satisfy this longing with worldly pleasures. Financial success, entertainment, sex, intoxicating substances, food, education, competition, and accolades can't fill the void. Each of these pleasures only reminds us that something is missing. These temporary pleasures satisfy our hunger for a moment, but they fail to quench our thirst that comes back time and again.

How can we find our way back?

In a word, Jesus.

It sounds like the Sunday school answer, and it is, but there is so much more depth in that one name, and most Christians are simply scratching the surface. Jesus did not come just to get us into heaven (although that's what most people latch onto). The story is so much better than that! Jesus came to reunite us to God, the Father. Jesus came to reunite heaven and earth. Jesus came to redeem all of creation. Jesus came to invite us to come home, to experience a blessed life.

Jesus came to *redefine* everything about our lives.

Jesus came to show us the way home and give us a blessed life until we get there.

Back to the Garden

This is the compelling story and message of the Bible. In the first two chapters, God creates paradise, creates mankind, and invites us to rule and reign with Him forever building the kingdom of God on earth. Then, tragically, mankind declared our independence from God. Our relationship with God and each other was destroyed. The rest of the Bible describes man trying to create heaven *without* God and God trying to reveal to man His heart and character.

God patiently endures our sin, independence, and the pain and suffering we have caused hoping we will see His heart and hear His invitation to *come home*, to be blessed. Finally, God goes all-in. He sends Jesus, His only son, to demonstrate a living example of God's character for us to follow and to redeem mankind. In the last two chapters of the Bible, God *has* redeemed all of creation.

Heaven and earth; God and man are reunited through the redemptive work of Christ, and we live with Him in paradise forever. Jesus came to make salvation available to all who put their trust in him.

When Jesus was here, he modeled and taught what life in the garden looks like. This is a life of humble dependence. The result? A life of blessing! That is the kind of relationship Jesus wants. He did not come to give us a list of rules.

The garden was not about rules but relationships. Jesus reduced the law to two relational directives; "Love the Lord your God with all your heart, soul, and mind… love your neighbor as yourself. The entire law and all the demands of the prophets are based on these two commands." (Matthew 22:36-40)

The Kingdom of God is not about rules, but relationships. Rules come with loopholes, but love comes with mercy, authenticity, peace, and hope! When we love God and love each other we begin to experience the abundant life Jesus longs for us to experience (John 10:10). We are living life redefined. This is what Jesus is describing in John 15. Jesus wants us to understand that everything we need in life is going to flow out of our relationship and connection with him. Jesus said, "If you abide in me you will bear much fruit, but apart from me you can do nothing." (John 15:5). This is the life we lost that Jesus came to restore! This is the *blessed* life Jesus came to give us.

I'm a pastor, so naturally, I am around a lot of Christians. If asked, most would say, "Of course I love Jesus." And I believe them.

They do love Jesus.

They love what Jesus has done for them.

They love who he is.

They love knowing they will be in heaven one day.

Usually, they love the church and all their church friends.

But that's kind of where it stops. It's a shallow kind of love.

Very few Christians can honestly describe a personal, conversational, and daily connection with Jesus. They know they need Jesus to go to heaven but are not sure what he could possibly do to help them with everyday life. In fact, when they look back over their Christian life, if they were completely honest, they may even admit, *when I have been in trouble I have prayed and prayed but God never answered me.* Unanswered prayer is a topic too broad for us to tackle here, but one reason God is not answering is that we have departed from Him. I do not mean we are no longer Christians, but what I am saying is that at some point, we started making independent decisions, calling the shots, created a mess, and are now trying to talk God into bailing us out. God is not into bailouts. God is into character building, and the pain of our independence is often the catalyst that drives us into humble dependence and abundant life. This has certainly been true for me.

This is the path to a blessed life!

Often people wonder, why is there so much pain and suffering in our world?

On a macro-level, man declared independence from God and invited sin, rebellion, evil, pain, and suffering into God's good creation. God created a perfect paradise without any pain and suffering, but mankind corrupted God's good creation. The suffering in our world is the result of our sin and rebellion.

On a micro-level, each of us must decide if we are going to allow Jesus to be king. Is he going to be in charge, or are we going to declare our independence, make our own choices, and build our own kingdom? We are all born with a sinful nature. We are born revolutionaries. We are born with a stubborn determination to be in charge.

Hopefully, at some point later in life, usually motivated by the pain we have experienced on a macro- or micro-level, through our independence and rebellion or the independence and rebellion in our world, we are humbled, broken, surrender, and learn to live in dependence on Christ. We invite Jesus to be our king. This begins our journey into a blessed life. Therefore, God patiently tolerates the pain and suffering in our world, with a broken heart, knowing our pain points us to Jesus and leads us into a blessed and eternal life (John 11:1-44).

We have all heard that Christianity is about "a relationship, not religion". What most mean by that is the way to heaven is through Jesus, not rules. This is true. Jesus is the only way to heaven, but cultivating a personal, tangible, conversational relationship with him now is the only way to experience a blessed life. This is what Jesus is describing in the Sermon on the Mount. Jesus came to redefine for us what a relationship with God should look like. Jesus came to invite us out of the emptiness of religion and into the fullness of abundant life in Christ.

This book is about how to find your way there—to find your way home.

PART I

Reconnect with God and People

Blessing

Redefined

J esus begins his ministry with a bang. You probably know the basics of Jesus's bio—he was born to Mary (a virgin) and Joseph in Bethlehem. The wise men came with gifts; Herod went on a rampage, and they fled to Egypt for safety. At some point, they made it back to Nazareth where Jesus was raised as the son of a carpenter. At age twelve, he taught in the temple and astonished the people there with his knowledge and wisdom. For nearly twenty years we don't know much about Jesus's life. But when it's time to begin his ministry, he starts with an intense forty-day period of prayer, fasting, and testing. Then, his wild-haired, camel-hair-wearing, locust-eating cousin baptizes him in the Jordan River.

His first miracle? Turning water into wine.

His first sermon? The Sermon on the Mount.

This very important sermon lays out Jesus's teaching on a variety of subjects. In this sermon, Jesus describes our relationship with him, each other, and our world. When Jesus climbed up the hillside to address the crowd on that first-century day, he looked out on primarily a Jewish audience. Most of these people were beaten down. They'd been occupied by the Roman empire, who took what they wanted and cruelly punished those who didn't play by the rules. The prophets had been silent for four hundred years, and the followers of Yahweh were beginning to lose hope.

One thing they had plenty of was religion.

The Jews were very religious, and their relationship with God and each other was all about rules. But when Jesus began to teach that afternoon, he turned everything they thought they knew about God on its head.

Jesus came to show them—to show us—that God wants much more for us than to struggle to obey a list of rules. Anyone can obey the rules yet hate the rule-giver. Wayward teenagers and shackled prisoners know this. Jesus knew the rules were important, but he is after more than just our obedience. He wants us to have a strong relationship with him and with each other, which eliminates most of the pain and suffering in our world.

The Jews understood *religion*; Jesus was about to give them a crash course on *relationship*.

The Sermon on the Mount is his first, longest, and most famous sermon. It lays the theological foundation for the rest of his life and ministry, and the groundwork for the Christian faith. He begins with what we call the *Beatitudes*. The Beatitudes describe our spiritual posture before God and each other. These Beatitudes are the foundation of a blessed life.

Just as the ten commandments begin by addressing our relationship with God and then describe how our relationship with God should impact our relationships with each other, the Beatitudes do the same.

The first four Beatitudes describe *our relationship with God*; the second four describe how our relationship with God impacts *the way we relate to each other.* It's only once our relationships with God and each other are healthy and growing that we are able to address the crucial ethical and moral questions of the day from a *relational* framework.

The teaching from the Sermon on the Mount helps us understand how each of these issues can be understood by filtering them through our love for God and our love for each other.

This is crucial for two reasons.

First, Jesus makes it clear that our first priority must be our relationship with God. If our relationship with God is strong, *He* changes our character and empowers us to love other people well. You don't have to be around people very long before you realize that some of them aren't always easy to love.

Second, this relational focus on both God *and* people illustrates the difference between Christianity and every other religious system. Religion compels us to work hard, follow the rules, and if you do enough, *maybe* you can earn a relationship with God.

It's like running a race without a finish line.

Jesus taught the opposite.

Jesus taught us to come to him just like we are, and he would change us *from the inside out.* This change means we would love him and he would fill our hearts with love for each other (Romans 5:1-5). We do not earn the right to be close to Jesus; Jesus did that for us by his death, resurrection, and indwelling presence. We do not work at loving each other, God *produces* His love for each other in our hearts. When we understand this, it sets our hearts free, takes the pressure to produce off, and leads us into new life, abundant life, a BLESSED life!

What Does it Mean to Be Blessed?

You may have heard this from a cashier after handing you your receipt: "Have a *blessed* day." You may have even said it to someone else. But have you ever wondered what that actually means?

The word blessed means happy. At the moment Jesus delivered the Sermon on the Mount, the Jews were anything but happy. They did not look or feel blessed. They were suffering under the harsh, immoral, and pagan rule of the Roman Empire. They were hopeless and discouraged. For the last 400 years, God had been silent.

In today's culture, Americans probably don't feel much different.

We are more prosperous, more entertained, overfed, oversexed and yet—when you look around—miserable. We are stressed, afraid, anxious, empty, isolated, angry, broke, and lost. If our political party isn't in office, we feel angry and oppressed. We fear missing out when we look at our social media feeds and see everyone else's blessings.

We can't hear God because the noise of culture drowns Him out.

We want hope and blessing but aren't sure where to find it.

This is where the Jews found themselves that day.

So when Jesus steps on the stage, the people pay attention.

Jesus begins his ministry with an announcement, a proclamation. It's wonderful news concerning the kingdom of God. It's an unspoken question that stirs at the heartfelt desire that every person longs for—a life of blessing.

Jesus begins his ministry by inviting us into a blessed life, a new life, a happy life!

Think about how refreshing that must have felt to a broken and oppressed people.

They had no idea what was coming next, but he must have hooked them with this promise.

Jesus wants us to have the same things: be blessed and experience kingdom living. But what does that look like today? For most people (and maybe for you too) a blessed life means a life of security, popularity, prosperity, and health. These things may be nice, but they aren't what Jesus had in mind.

Jesus *redefined* what it means to be blessed.

Jesus is not offering a superficial, circumstantial blessing. Jesus had a new definition of blessed: *a deep sense of wellbeing, satisfaction, and contentment that comes from having a thriving relationship with Christ and cultivating healthy relationships with other people.*

Think about your own life for a moment. How might that kind of blessing change your life? What if you knew *exactly* how to begin your day in God's presence and experience His peace all day long? What if each of your relationships with the people in your life were healthy, vibrant, and thriving?

How might that change your life?

It's what Jesus would do for the next three years with his disciples. Every day they would walk *with him* and experience a relationship *with each other.* This would change everything.

You see, the Christian life is not about working for him or knowing about him but being WITH him. When we are with him, he works in and through us. When we are with him, we know him and people see him in us. When we are with him, we begin to relate to others the way he relates to us.

The blessing is not in doing but in being.

The blessing is the experience of walking with him.

The blessing is new life, the power of Christ at work in us.

Jesus is emphatic—*nine times*—he invites us into a new, blessed life in Christ!

Christ's words in this invitation, expose the emptiness of our pursuits. How many Americans would honestly describe themselves as blessed? Today we live like kings, and yet we feel empty, isolated, angry, disappointed, desperate, and lost.

We have luxuries today that were unimaginable in the first century. Electricity, air conditioning, indoor plumbing, refrigerators, cars, internet, cell phones, and beautiful houses with green grass in the yard are the norm. We have access to free public education, health care, hospitals, grocery stores, and unlimited entertainment. Yet deep down, we often feel empty, alone, and desperate. No matter what or how much we manage to stuff in our souls, we leak, feel empty, and the hunger pains remain.

What is missing? Where is the blessing?

Into our discontent, Jesus describes a life of blessing.

Jesus also models, over the next three years, what this life looks like. Humble dependence on the Father, unshakable strength in his purpose, plan, and power, and vibrant, giving, serving relationships with others.

This was the blessing.

Jesus was poor, misunderstood, falsely-accused, under constant spiritual attack, rejected, and crucified, yet because of his connection to the Father, he had peace of mind. He was blessed!

I know what you're thinking.

Well, sure he was blessed. Jesus was God, which is much different from me.

How can I experience this blessed life?

I'm glad you asked.

Jesus's Big Idea

The rest of Section 1 is going to unpack the Beatitudes from Jesus's Sermon on the Mount. It may turn your thinking inside out and upside down. That's good. That's how the Word of God changes your life.

But before we look at each of these Beatitudes, let's first ask the question *what is the big idea?* What is the overarching point Jesus is trying to make? What kind of life is the Christian life, a blessed life? The blessed life is a life of humble dependence that produces unexpected blessings.

Religion is about *my* effort, *my* works, *my* discipline, and what *I* can produce.

As Mr. Self-sufficient and Independent, this kind of religion worked for me because it was something I could control.

That's not the Christian life.

It's time to face the facts—what if everything you *think* you know about faith is wrong?

This may be jarring, but trust me; I've seen it for years, and when people allow Jesus to redefine what they know about faith, it's life-changing.

Jesus came because he was *pleading* for people to realize there was more to life than simply following the rules. The secret to a blessed life is coming to the end of yourself. It's recognizing that no matter how hard you try, and no matter what you accomplish, it does not satisfy.

Like a frustrated child who finally admits he needs a parent's help, you must give up to discover the blessing of a father's strong and generous touch. When you humble yourself and learn to live in dependence, you discover a new life. And in this new life, something wonderful happens—the pressure is off. Forgiven, united with

Christ, and walking with him, he produces his life in you, and you are blessed.

All of our striving only moves us further from God and hardens our hearts. All of our self-accomplishment builds walls around our souls. We must tear down these walls and accept God's gracious invitation to live a blessed life in Him.

In the Beatitudes, Jesus begins by describing the condition of a person's heart, the spiritual posture of those who live in him. Jesus is describing what it looks like to yield to him and allow the Holy Spirit to transform your life from the inside out.

Humility, brokenness, surrender, and dependence are the steps into new life and a new relationship with him. Once we taste this new life in Christ, it radically changes how we begin to relate to other people. We begin to experience unexpected mercy towards those who are hurting, a desire for authenticity, a passion for peace, and a willingness to value what is eternal over what is temporary.

Our relationships with God and each other begin to prosper. This empowers us to address the moral, social, and ethical issues of our day. It allows us to experience a blessed life and share that life with others. Most importantly, it equips us to *become like Jesus*. Jesus teaches us how we can be profoundly, deeply, and spiritually satisfied in our relationship with him and maintain this state throughout life's inevitable disappointments and suffering.

It's time to climb the mountain and sit at the feet of the Master. Are you ready?

It's time to be blessed.

CHAPTER ONE

The Poor in Spirit

Blessed are the poor in spirit, for theirs
is the kingdom of heaven.

Here's a quick exercise for you: think of five adjectives you'd hope best describe you at the end of your life. Did you write them down? Now, look at your list. Was *poor* written anywhere on your list? How about *insignificant, not highly regarded,* or even *looked down upon?*

I'm guessing that none of those made your list.

If you're like most people, those descriptors wouldn't even be found in your top-50.

So why does Jesus begin his most famous sermon with these words: *Blessed are the poor in spirit.* To understand the why you have to first understand the what.

Being poor in spirit means recognizing that apart from the redeeming work of Christ, you are spiritually bankrupt. This is not an easy thing to admit. This challenges our cultural understanding that all people are morally good. The truth is, we are born sinners. All people are born bad, evil, self-centered, and immoral.

God wants to produce humility in each of us. He can't do that when we lie about who we are.

In Romans 3:10-12, Paul says, "No one is righteous, no not even one. No one is truly wise; no one is seeking God. All have turned away; all have become useless. No one does good, not a single one."

Jesus said, "It is from within, out of a person's heart, that evil thoughts come—sexual immorality, theft, murder, adultery, greed, malice, deceit, lewdness, envy, slander, arrogance and folly. All these evils come from inside and defile a person" (Mark 7:21-23). If you have the courage to look at the deepest part of your soul, you understand the truth in these words.

But that takes courage and a willingness to own up to your shortcomings.

Most people would rather gloss over them and present an inauthentic version of themselves that they think the world wants to see. This isn't the way to God's blessing. His blessing does not come from *denying* our wickedness but by understanding and experiencing the transforming power of God's grace.

When we understand the depth of our depravity, we can appreciate the beauty of the Gospel and begin moving toward humble dependence. This dependence *upon* God (being poor in spirit) becomes the foundation of our relationship *with* God and people.

Having a proper understanding of our spiritual condition without Christ and all that Christ has won for us through his death and resurrection produces humility, gratitude, and wonder as we discover the depth of God's love, grace, mercy, and generosity.

This produces worship in our hearts.

This is what it means to be humble in heart and poor in spirit.

In this selfie generation, we've become impressed with ourselves. We stand so close to the mirror that the glory of God is hidden from our sight. We worship ourselves—we look to ourselves for identity, security, and happiness—but if we are honest, we find the burden of playing God exhausting.

In Romans 1:18-32, Paul describes what happens when we reject God and attempt to find or create a blessed life without Him. He describes how our vain pursuit, independent of God, has produced a curse not a blessing, death not life, bondage not freedom, and rage not joy. This is why when you look at our world you see and can even feel the rage of our frustration and disappointment. In the words of the cultural philosophers U2, "We still haven't found what we're looking for."

Jesus says stop striving, stop trying to produce what you are incapable of producing. Empty yourself and turn to me. In essence, see yourself for what you are and *give me room to work*.

Religion says if you work a little harder and do a little better you can please God.

We like that because it makes us feel in control.

However, the Bible teaches the opposite. It says my good works are like filthy rags (Isaiah 64:6). Apart from Jesus, my good works are an expression of my independence and rebellion. It is my way of saying to Jesus, just like a small child, "I can do it all by myself!"

It's funny in children, not so much in people who should know better.

You see, good deeds are a way for me to exalt myself over God. They put the focus on me and make me the hero of the story. But if I am going to be blessed, Jesus says, I have to come to the end of myself. I must come to the place where I realize that despite my religious activity or my best efforts, without Him, I am nothing.

Religious activity and good works may impress people, but if they are not the fruit of our relational connection with God, they become a self-imposed barrier and overlook the condition of our hearts.

We may long and beg for God's blessing, but God's presence is optional. However, if we humble ourselves and turn back to God, if we admit our bankruptcy and cry out to Him, He will bless us.

Sometimes this can be a painful process.

Lessons in Humility

This is one of the real dangers of religion and what Jesus came to combat. Religion convinces us we are good. With religion, we feel like we have done well, especially compared to our non-religious friends. The problem is, rather than humble dependence, religion creates prideful *independence*, which becomes a barrier between us and God and robs us of a blessed life.

This is one of the dangers of American culture. You can live an immoral, self-centered life for years and experience "success" without ever recognizing the condition of your soul and the long-term consequences of your pride.

But this has been going on for as long as people have walked the earth.

We see this pattern throughout the Bible in the lives of the biblical characters. Most of these men started out like me. They did not know how to walk with God, so their relationships were a mess. Rather than humble dependence, they were prideful and independent. This pride led to their fall. Then through their suffering (poorness of spirit) they learned humility and dependence, and despite their trials and suffering, began to experience a blessed life.

Joseph was the spoiled, favored son of Jacob. This made him proud and mouthy. He was a dreamer, ambitious, and chosen by God. However, he was immature. By not learning to walk with God, he damaged his relationship with his brothers. His judgment towards them drove a wedge in their relationship. You probably remember the story—Joseph ends up being sold into slavery, his beautiful coat of many colors covered in blood.

I am sure Joseph asked himself the question, *What have I done?*

Over time, he began to see how his pride and disrespect for his older brothers led him to this place. This once arrogant young man reached rock bottom and realized he desperately needed God's grace.

The first step into a blessed life is not physical freedom but spiritual freedom, not pride but humility. Joseph needed to be freed from pride before he could be freed from slavery. His pride produced his bondage and blocked his blessing. It does the same for us until we become poor in spirit.

Moses was rescued by God as a baby and raised in the Palace of Pharaoh. Growing up in the palace provided Moses with a world-class education and military training. He was connected, influential, wealthy, and powerful. However, his privileged upbringing also had a downside. It made him arrogant and intolerant, religious but unspiritual, impulsive, and independent.

A young, strong, zealous man, he witnessed an Egyptian soldier mistreating a Jew and reacted without thinking. In a moment of passion, he killed this soldier and was forced to flee the country as a fugitive.

In the years that follow, Moses goes from being a prince of Egypt to a lowly, unknown shepherd. Day after day and night after night as he watched his sheep and contemplated the turn his life had taken, he found himself asking the question, *What have I done?*

When we do something foolish and life falls apart, we all ask this question. In those quiet moments, Moses began to see his arrogance, pride, and independence—not as assets, but as liabilities. He assumed God was finished with him, but God was just getting started. Moses was becoming poor in spirit.

Even walking in-person with Jesus, you can still fail to be poor in spirit. Peter was proud and independent. At the Passover Meal, he boasted, "Even if all these other disciples fall away, I will never fall away; I am prepared to die for you." But later that night after Jesus was arrested, Peter denied him three times and was exposed. As Jesus looked into Peter's eyes, Peter must have been thinking *What have I done?*

Those next hours must have been torture for Peter as he looked at himself with shame. His arrogance and his boasting were broken as humility and broken spirit flooded in. Peter thought he was finished, but God was just getting started. After the resurrection, a humble Peter reconnects with Jesus and becomes the Rock of the early church and begins to understand the blessed life.

Paul was a religious zealot, a Pharisee, a defender of Judaism, and a persecutor of the church. Paul traveled from city to city to arrest, punish, and kill Christians. He was an international terrorist and proud of it.

However, on his way to the city of Damascus, Paul was surrounded by a blinding light and was about to make a shocking, life-changing discovery that would break his arrogance and pride and force humility on him in an instant. As the light shone upon him, Paul fell to the ground and Jesus asked, "Saul! Saul! Why are you persecuting me?" Paul does not know who is speaking to him, so he asks, "Who are you, Lord?" A voice, out of the blinding light responds, "I am Jesus, the one you are persecuting!"

In that moment, time stood still. Paul's mind was racing. *Could this be real? Am I dreaming? Have I gone crazy? Is Jesus, the one I have been persecuting, actually the Messiah?* Jesus told Paul to go to the city and he would receive instructions about what to do next. On that long, quiet ride Paul was in shock, asking the question, *What have I done?*

God showed him the depth of his depravity, his pride, his violence, and his judgment, and once his eyes were open, poorness in spirit flooded in. This self-confessed "chief of sinners" now had a new life and a new blessing to pursue. His mission: share the Gospel with the world.

In Luke 15, Jesus tells the story of the prodigal son. In his pride, this son rebelled against his father, declared his independence, left home, and began indulging in immorality. After squandering his inheritance, he finds himself working for a pig farmer. He is so hungry he is longing to eat the pig's food. He must have been asking, *What have I done?*

The once-proud young Jewish man is completely humiliated and decides to return to his father. He is poor in spirit. When he finally crosses the field to stand before the father he rejected, he says, "Father, I am not worthy to be your son." In response to his son's humility, the father covered his filth with his robe, trusted him with authority and responsibility, and threw a party to celebrate his return.

These stories show us what it's like to become poor in spirit and serve as a reminder that it's a continual battle. Rebellion and independence always drive us away from the Father. Sometimes our rebellion and independence are expressed in our immorality and sometimes our good works, but either way, we find ourselves a long way from home.

The Christian life is a life of humble dependence. God wants to bless us, but we must come to the end of ourselves, return home, and throw ourselves on His mercy. But how do we come to the end of ourselves?

I learned that lesson the hard way.

When I left home to attend seminary, I was the opposite of poor in spirit. In fact, I arrived feeling pretty good about myself. I was more zealous than most. I was bold, courageous, strong, and passionate. I possessed a great work ethic. I was a natural leader, and I loved church.

Church had provided me a platform to lead and excel.

Ministry earned me the respect and admiration of others.

I loved Jesus and was grateful for my salvation, but my life was a façade.

Despite all my efforts, I did not know how to have a personal relationship with him. I did not understand the importance of connecting with him each day. I had no idea how to follow his lead. I couldn't see how my relationship with Jesus impacted my other relationships.

Jesus was my job.

From outward appearances, I had it all together.

Inside, I had the shallowest of relationships with Jesus, was fiercely independent, battling a secret porn addiction, and critical and judgmental towards those who did not match my religious zeal. I was just like the Pharisees that Jesus criticizes in Matthew 23.

Outside, I looked great; inside, I was a complete mess.

I had the same problem in my marriage. The relational issues we have with Jesus will manifest themselves in all our relationships. I loved my wife and enjoyed being a husband. I thought I was working hard to do what husbands are supposed to do. I was a good provider, I helped around the house, and I was committed to our marriage. But marriage is more than just doing the right things.

Since I did not know how to connect with Tina's heart, she felt unloved.

We were married, but to her, it felt like we were just roommates. We lived in the same home, but we were living separate, independent lives, and it was killing her. When my marriage fell apart and the illusion was shattered, I realized how relationally bankrupt I really was.

It left me thinking, *What have I done?*

Without Jesus I was nothing; I had nothing.

It was the first time I really understood what it meant to be *poor in spirit.*

Sometimes it takes seeing your world blow up to drop the pretense and embrace authenticity.

From then on, I stopped faking it. I made a commitment to kick my hypocrisy to the curb.

I'd been trying to live a perfect life; now I wanted to live a transparent life.

I knew that without Jesus I was going to lose everything that was important to me. Perhaps you've found yourself there before. Maybe that is where you find yourself now—desperate, broken, and humiliated. It's not a fun place to be, but that's exactly where you find God.

The Kingdom of God does not belong to the well-meaning but to the desperate.

Humility is rarely our default. It's much easier to slip into pride, but pride and independence eventually lead to our downfall. If you are serious about becoming like Jesus, it's time to be broken in spirit.

Jesus says the poor in spirit will get a taste of the kingdom of heaven here on earth. It comes through our union and fellowship with Christ in the person and work of the Holy Spirit. Although we are not back in paradise yet, and things are not yet as they will be, we *can* experience a taste of God's kingdom on earth if we learn to empty ourselves of pride and walk with Him.

Kingdom living is not just a future promise but a present reality for the poor in spirit. Those who recognize their spiritual bankruptcy and throw themselves on the mercy of God can rest in His grace and experience a blessed life. When you humble yourself and learn to trust God's grace the pressure is off.

You do not have to perform.

You can rest in His grace and trust Him to produce his life in you.

And that strengthens every relationship.

That leads to a blessed life.

CHAPTER TWO

The Mourners

Blessed are those who mourn, for they will be comforted.

Two of the hardest words in the world to say are *I'm sorry*. It's not difficult to see why when you consider what the last chapter was about.

Pride is like walking in quicksand. It makes everything we do (or hope to do) more difficult, and saying *I'm sorry* when you've made a mistake is right at the top of the list. Yet these two words have so much power to heal, mend, and fix broken relationships.

This starts with our relationship with God.

The first step to becoming like Jesus is to recognize your need to be poor in spirit. I talked about how to do that in the last chapter. That may help you open the door to the Kingdom of God, but it takes more than that to walk through that door.

When Jesus says, *blessed are those who mourn*, he's talking about people who have replaced their pride with humility—but then move a step further. They mourn the mess they have made, the pain they've created in their lives and in the lives of others. They are blessed because they do not make excuses for their spiritual condition. They no longer try to justify their independence, immaturity, immorality, or insensitivity.

Saying *I'm sorry* means they own their failures and are brokenhearted over them.

Blessed are the broken.

The first-century Jews lived under the Roman empire in a culture of immorality, oppression, abuse, greed, lust, and violence. Everywhere they looked were the pagan gods of Rome, and the Jews had been assimilated into this Roman culture. They lost their spiritual vitality; however, this apathy was camouflaged by the comfort and prosperity that Rome provided.

The Jewish religious leaders were not broken at all; rather, they were spoiled, proud, and hypocritical. It's no wonder they didn't like Jesus (and he wasn't too fond of them). Jesus said, "O Jerusalem, Jerusalem, the city that kills the prophets and stones God's messengers! How often I have wanted to gather your children together as a hen protects her chicks beneath her wings, but you wouldn't let me" (Matthew 23:37).

Hard-hearted people rarely need comforting.

Whether it's blindness, self-deceit, or ignorance, they think they have it all together, while nothing could be further from the truth.

In Jesus's day, the people who'd been corrupted by the culture were comfortable, and as a result, their heart was hardened to their sin. Our culture today is not very different. Our comfort, safety, and prosperity often blind us to our true spiritual condition. In Matthew 9:36 it says when "Jesus saw the crowds, he was moved with compassion for them, because they were harassed and helpless, like sheep without a shepherd." Lost sheep may know they are separated from the flock, but they aren't smart enough to see the danger this puts them in.

Lessons in Brokenness

After five months of marriage, I thought things were going well. I was working hard in seminary, my job, and to be (what I thought was) a good husband. The achiever in me was firing on all cylinders.

So when Tina told me she did not love me or want to be married and would never be in the ministry, it was like I had stepped on a landmine I hadn't seen. With that one statement, everything that I valued appeared to be lost.

My marriage—lost.

My ministry—lost.

My reputation—lost.

What else did I have?

And so I hit rock bottom.

Tina and I had dated for four years before marriage. During those four years, we unhealthily swept our issues under the rug. In fact, the first time we were engaged, Tina called off our engagement over these same issues. Now, I was in a mess of my own making, and I did not know what to do. In my brokenness, I suddenly realized I was in over my head. Rock bottom is one of the best places to realize that without God's help you are not going to make it.

Until we get to the end of our rope, we never learn to let go and trust Jesus. However, when we turn to Jesus, broken over the mess we have made and the pain we have caused, God comes to comfort and restore us. That's what it means to be comforted.

We find that in our weakness, His strength is perfected (2 Corinthians 12:7-10). We begin to embrace a life of humble dependence (1 Peter 5:5-7). *God, if you will still have me, I am yours!* This is the prayer of those who mourn.

It was certainly my prayer. I was broken over my spiritual and psychological condition, the mess I had made, and the pain my wife was experiencing. I was mourning the death of my fake, religious, hypocritical, failure of a life. I was mourning the loss of my dream to be a pastor.

But as 2 Corinthians 7:10 says, "Godly sorrow leads to repentance."

I was certainly sorrowful, and I was working on understanding repentance.

Sometimes that takes time.

If we are going to live a blessed life, we must ask God to produce in us godly sorrow over our sin and the pain it has caused. It's as true for us now as it was for the men and women in the Bible.

Imagine how difficult it would have been to go from being the loved, favored, spoiled, protected, and pampered son to slave and prisoner in a foreign land. This was Joseph. From the highest of highs to the lowest of lows, Joseph had lost everything—family, homeland, status, name, and culture.

His pride created a lot of pain, for himself but also for those he loved. His father and mother were broken-hearted. His brothers were full of guilt, shame, regret, and fear knowing they'd gone too far. They probably wondered if their brother was still alive and had nightmares about how he was being treated.

I suspect Joseph spent many nights during those fourteen years as a slave mourning over all that his arrogance and his boasting cost him. He must have prayed over and over, *I'm so sorry!*

This is the prayer of those who mourn.

In those quiet moments, Joseph encountered the comforter. He could feel the love and mercy of God. He was not alone in this prison. The bars kept him caged, but his heart was freed. As he humbled himself and mourned the condition of his soul and the consequences of his pride, he began to experience the blessing of God's comfort.

Because of his actions, Moses lost everything too. It must be very difficult to go from being treated like a king, where everyone around you is literally at your service, to becoming a fugitive on the run. When he finally stopped running, he became a shepherd to a bunch of smelly sheep in the middle of the desert. Gone was the comfortable life of pleasure, fame, importance, family, security, purpose, and freedom.

Moses, I am sure, spent many nights over those forty years weeping and mourning his losses and praying, *I'm so sorry!* Moses was brokenhearted over his sin and the pain he caused. In those quiet moments, as Moses humbled himself and mourned the consequences of his sin, he encountered the comforter. He could feel the love and mercy of God. He may have been miles away from Egypt, but he was not alone in this wilderness. He was in the middle of God's blessing.

How much more broken can you be than going from one of Jesus's inner circle to denying you even know him and watching him face a gruesome death on a Roman cross? I can only imagine how embarrassed and humiliated Peter must have been after denying Christ. Just a few hours earlier, Peter was boasting about his courage and willingness to lay down his life; now, he felt as if he would die of sorrow and shame.

In a moment of weakness, he denied Jesus his King and turned his back on all he'd witnessed in the past three years. Have you ever said something without thinking and wished you could go back and un-say it? I suspect he played that moment of denial over and over in his mind trying to process the shame, guilt, and regret he was feeling. He was trying to comprehend the pain Jesus must have experienced.

As his brokenness nearly crushed him, I suspect he kept saying over and over, *I'm so sorry!* Peter thought he was all alone, but as he humbled himself and mourned his sin and betrayal, he encountered the comforter. In this moment of brokenness, the comforter drew near and began rebuilding the rock upon which He'd build His church.

Then there's Paul.

He was the straight-A student, teacher's pet, who knew it all and was filled with pride.

He saw Christianity as something to be eradicated and Christ-followers as someone to be destroyed. In the literal blink of an eye, everything he thought he knew about his life and its purpose changed.

The murderer met the master on the road to Damascus, and while his eyes were blinded, his heart was broken. I can only imagine how brokenhearted Paul was as he slowly made his way to Damascus, shuffling along and dependent upon his companions for his health and safety.

Deep in the darkness, Paul must have realized his pride and religious zeal had blinded him to the truth and caused him to do the unspeakable to the Lord's followers. He probably had trouble erasing the images from his mind of Christians crying out for mercy, or worse, praying for him as he and his band of zealots tortured and murdered them.

How could he have been so blind? How could he be responsible for so much pain?

Paul probably assumed his blindness was God's just punishment for his violence against Christ's followers. As Paul sat in darkness, weeping over his brutality, I suspect he could hear the words of Stephen ringing in his ears, "Lord, don't charge them with this sin!" as he fell to his knees and died (Acts 7:60, 8:1).

In the darkness, Paul's heart must have begun to cry out, *I'm so sorry!*

As he sat alone in darkness, humbled by his encounter with Christ, broken over his pride and violence, he began to feel the presence of another. That night Paul encountered the comforter. He could feel the love and mercy of God. He could not comprehend, after all the pain he caused, how could God... He could not even finish that sentence, but he could not deny his experience. It was as if God himself was present, around Him, holding him, and encouraging him.

You might not have been sold into slavery like Joseph, a murderer like Moses, a betrayer like Peter, or a terrorist like Paul, but you probably know where you've fallen short. Have you ever stopped and mourned over your own spiritual condition? Have you ever been broken over the pain you have created?

In 1997, as I sat in my apartment morning after morning, pondering the mess I was in, I was heartbroken. I was prideful, unspiritual, independent, insecure, and immoral. For the first time, I could see so clearly the poor condition of my soul. I was exposed.

For years I *performed* to cover my sin and earn the praise of those around me. Now there was no more hiding. I was also worried about Tina and the pain she was experiencing. In this dark place, I was unsure if our marriage would survive this crisis. Tina had trusted me with her heart, her life, and her future, but I had made so many promises that were now broken.

At that moment, I realized I did not have the character necessary to be the husband she needed and that I had promised to be. My pride and immorality had come at a cost greater than I could bear. My ministry and marriage were both in serious jeopardy.

In my brokenness, I found myself praying, *I'm so sorry!*

I wish I could tell you that after I prayed a powerful bolt of lightning came down from heaven and miraculously, instantly healed my marriage and ministry. It did not happen that way for me, and I do not think it happens that way for most people.

Character takes time to build.

It takes even longer to *rebuild*.

Relationships take time to heal and mature.

However, I was humbled and broken, and that's where God can work best. As I prayed, in the midst of my hopelessness, I began to experience His supernatural comfort. Although it appeared my marriage and ministry were over, I had an inexplicable peace, hope, strength, and faith.

I began to realize I am not alone.

Over the years, I've seen this happen time and again—in brokenness is blessing.

Recently, I was talking to a pastor friend. Over the last two years, he has made a mess of his life and caused a lot of pain to the people he loves and his congregation. As we talked on the phone, he wept openly over all he has lost. He is truly a humble and broken man now. It is emotionally difficult to see someone you care about so broken, and I do not know if he will ever regain all that he has lost.

But this I do know.

Jesus says my friend is blessed. Jesus says blessed are the humble and the broken. My friend is learning to find comfort in Christ even through his pain. He is learning that he is not alone and can never be so far from God that he can't find his way back.

In the midst of his despair, he is beginning to taste the blessing.

If you've been broken, take heart. Mourn. But look for the blessing.

The comforter is there waiting to take you in.

CHAPTER THREE

The Surrendered

Blessed are the meek, for they will inherit the earth.

Face it—no one likes to give up. It seems to go against our nature. After all, giving up, throwing in the towel, and backing down are hard to do—especially when you are competitive and want to win. But as admirable as it is to push into the face of adversity with a *Never Surrender!* attitude, it isn't always wise.

That's what makes the third Beatitude stand out so much.

After introducing the idea of being poor in spirit (having humility) and mourning (brokenness), Jesus introduces another counterintuitive concept—meekness.

You can almost hear the grumbles going through the crowd as they listened to Jesus that day.

The word meekness does not mean weakness; rather, it is power under control. An army that pulls back from a fight to establish a greater tactical advantage isn't weak; it's using its power under control. It is making a choice to *not engage* now so it can engage later.

When Jesus says blessed are the meek, he means this: having enough humility and being motivated by your brokenness to bring your life under the authority of Christ. When we see the condition of our heart without Jesus and the sin and pain we have caused, we naturally want Jesus to take the lead!

That is tactical surrender, and it makes all the difference.

Lessons in Surrender

I have a very large Labrador retriever named Jake. When I say very large, I mean it. He weighs 110 pounds, so as you can imagine he is very strong. When I walk him, if he decides to run away or chase a cat or a rabbit, I doubt I could hold him back.

However, years ago I took him to a dog trainer for a week of doggy boot camp. When I picked him up, Jake was a different dog. He was very obedient to every command, so I asked the trainer, "What's your secret?" He explained that when he first gets a dog, there is a power struggle. The dog and the trainer are trying to figure out who is in charge. So he puts a training collar on the dog which administers a small electric pulse when the dog does not obey. He said it only takes hitting that button two or three times before the dog decides *I am not in charge; I will obey.*

The dog may be bigger and stronger, but the pain quickly produces meekness and power under control.

If your life is like mine, I'm sure you can relate.

In 1996, I went off to seminary full of zeal, promise, and pride. By the spring of 1997, I was humiliated, broken, and surrendered. My zeal, hard work, and religious activity had failed me. I was a seminary dropout with a failing marriage who did not know what to do.

When Tina and I moved back to Wilmington, I met Dr. Bill Bennett. Dr. Bennett was a semi-retired pastor, a Chaplain at the seminary, and author of several books. He had made a commitment to spend the final chapter of his life and ministry mentoring young pastors. I was introduced to Dr. Bennett a few months before dropping out, and I was on my way to his house to meet him formally. My hope was that he would disciple me and help me rebuild my marriage and ministry. That night I explained my situation to Dr. Bennett and humbly asked for his help.

There was a long moment of silence as he looked me in the eyes.

Finally, he asked me three questions: First, *Are you serious about changing?* Second, *Will you be a good student?* Finally, *Are you willing to be taught and learn discipline for your life?*

At that moment I had nowhere else to turn. My life was a train wreck. In my desperation, I agreed to do whatever he asked of me. I had no idea what I was getting myself into. We began meeting most mornings at 5 A.M. I wasn't sure I had *ever* been up at 5 A.M. For that matter, I wasn't even sure if God was up at 5 A.M., but I was determined to be meek and surrendered. If that meant waking up before God, then so be it. I was serious about getting my life back on track, so I was willing to surrender control of my life and my sleep schedule. My plans had failed, and I needed a new plan if I was going to salvage my marriage and ministry.

This is what Jesus is describing when he talks about surrender and meekness. It means coming to the end of ourselves and getting to the place where we realize that my strategy, my plans, my effort have failed, and I need Jesus.

We see this pattern over and over in the lives of many of the leaders God uses. God always brings them to a place of surrender. Often leaders "lead" for years, asking God to bless their ideas while trying to get Jesus to follow them. Eventually, they learn that Jesus wants to take the lead. Sadly, Jesus often has to allow pain, trials, or a crisis to break us of our independence so that he can lead us.

It's hard to think of much more of a trial than being sold into slavery by your family. To his mom and dad, Joseph was the favorite. He was protected, educated, and pampered at home while his brothers worked hard in the sun. Even his clothing signified his place of privilege, and every time they saw his many-colored coat walk by, his brothers were reminded that he was special while they were not. He was full of pride, and it showed.

God did have a special plan in mind for Joseph, but it was going to require meekness before it could come to pass. After being sold into slavery, Joseph's carefully ordered life was a series of ups and downs. He became a servant in the house of Potiphar, a high-ranking Egyptian leader. It was not long before Potiphar saw Joseph's potential, so he placed him in charge of his household. Suddenly, things were looking up for Joseph.

Then they fell again. Potiphar's wife attempted to seduce Joseph, and when he rejected her offer, she accused him of rape. This false accusation landed him in prison, and it appeared his dream was dead and God was far away.

I suspect as he sat alone in his prison cell, year after year, God began to speak to Joseph in a still, small voice. God was showing Joseph his own heart and bringing him to a place of surrender. The previous fourteen years and all his hard work had gotten him nowhere.

Would he die in prison?

Was God paying attention?

In those quiet moments, Joseph must have given up. There, he was broken, and when you are broken, you learn to surrender. Joseph became meek. He could see how easy it was to be prideful; he could see the pain he caused, and he was wondering *How do I keep from making a mistake like this again?*

The answer: meekness, surrender to God.

Have you ever done the right thing for the wrong reason?

Moses could relate.

He was doing a good thing—defending God's children. Ultimately, he *would* become the defender of Israel, but this was not God's time nor God's way. In his arrogance, Moses acted out independently and created a mess.

God has created us all with strengths, talents, natural gifts, and supernatural gifts.

We each have a story, education, and experience, and God wants to leverage all of that for the kingdom. But meekness means you realize His kingdom does not depend on our ability, but on His power.

Moses had tremendous ability and potential, but he had to learn to wait on God's timing. Israel's future was in God's hands. During those 40 years in the wilderness, Moses was humbled and broken. Moses could see how his immaturity led to his exile and wondered, *How do I avoid getting into that situation again?* Moses must have found himself surrendering: *God, I want you to be in charge. Call the shots. I have created a mess. I surrender my life to you!*

Then one day, Moses encountered God in a burning bush, and everything changed.

Peter was a take-charge leader.

He was an *act first, think second* kind of personality. He was the first to get out of the boat in a storm (Matthew 14), the first to declare Jesus as the Son of God (Matthew 16), the first to proclaim his courage (Matthew 26:35), and the first to pull out his sword (Matthew 26:51).

He was also the first to deny Jesus...multiple times and to different people (Matthew 26:70-74). I suspect as Peter sat weeping (Matthew 26:75) his world was spinning. When you rush to action, you have to be prepared for the consequences. So Peter sat there with his confidence shaken, his reputation destroyed, and his pride broken.

Jesus was crucified, eliminating any hope of making things right.

Peter must have cried bitter tears of sorrow—until Sunday rolled around.

Can you imagine the scene?

Three days later, when the women reported to Peter and the other disciples that the stone was rolled away and the tomb was empty, Peter took off to see for himself. Why wouldn't he? He was Peter. Later that day, they encountered the resurrected Lord. Jesus was alive!

A few days later, as Peter and some of the disciples were coming in from a night of fishing, they heard someone calling from the shore. When Peter realized it was Jesus, he immediately jumped into the water and headed for shore.

After breakfast, Jesus pulled Peter aside and asked him three times: "Peter, do you love me?"

Jesus knew Peter was taking his betrayal hard and wanted to reassure him.

I suspect in that moment it was all Peter could do to remain standing. Maybe he fell to his knees, head down, hot tears running down his face. Peter was strong, but finally his strength was gone. He was humble, broken, and surrendered. Peter was meek and ready for Jesus to lead.

Suddenly, Peter was right where he needed to be.

Paul was unusually gifted and zealous. He describes his former life in Judaism this way: "I was circumcised when I was eight days old. I am a pure-blooded citizen of Israel and a member of the tribe of Benjamin—a real Hebrew if there ever was one! I was a member of the Pharisees, who demanded the strictest obedience to the Jewish law. I was so zealous that I harshly persecuted the church. And as for righteousness, I obeyed the law without fault (Philippians 3:5-6).

I do not know any pastor who would dare make such bold claims.

They may have been true, but they were borne out of Paul's immense pride.

Paul *was* exceptional. However, his independent zeal brought him to the Damascus Road and face-to-face with the resurrected Christ. In that moment, Paul made a shocking discovery—all his zeal and achievement were not only wasted, they were working in *direct opposition* to the Kingdom of God.

Just imagine how devastating that discovery must have been for a man who was so proud, self-sufficient, and independent. As Paul sat in darkness, pondering the fact that all his work had actually *opposed* God, at some point, I believe Paul got down on his knees and asked Jesus to be in charge of his life.

He surrendered:

I once thought these things were valuable (his achievements), but now I consider them worthless because of what Christ has done. Yes, everything else is worthless when compared with the *infinite value* of knowing Christ Jesus my Lord. For his sake I have discarded everything else, counting it all as garbage, so that I could gain Christ and become one with him. I no longer count on my own righteousness through obeying the law; rather, I become righteous through faith in Christ. For God's way of making us right with himself depends on faith. I want to know Christ and experience the mighty power that raised him from the dead. I want to suffer with him, sharing in his death, so that one way or another I will experience the resurrection from the dead (Philippians 3:7-11)!

Paul was humbled and broken. He came to a place in his life that he considered his life nothing compared to the "surpassing value" of knowing Christ. He became meek. Jesus was his King!

It's tough to give up, because surrendering goes against our human nature.

But with faith, that's the only way you can find the blessing.

Have you ever come to the place where you can honestly say, *Jesus, I want you to be in charge of everything in my life?* Take charge of my mind, my schedule, my money, my sex life, my relationships, and my future.

We are by nature so independent, but as we learn to trust and follow him, we discover his way is best. Jesus came to give us an abundant, blessed life (John 10:10), but we have to learn to let him lead. When you retreat into the comfort of his embrace, you recognize the safety and security it provides.

When I was a small child I learned a song that went like this: *Is there anything I can do dear Lord, is there anything I can do? I am willing to be used dear Lord, is there anything I can do?* The song continues with two more verses; *is there anything I can be?* and *is there anywhere I can go?*

What if we were to all make this song our prayer? *If there is anything I can do, anything I can be, or anywhere I can go, I am willing to be used, dear Lord. My life is yours.*

Blessed are the meek, they will inherit the earth.

CHAPTER FOUR

The Hungry

Blessed are those who hunger and thirst for
righteousness, for they will be filled.

When you are poor in spirit, you understand humility.
When you are in mourning, you understand brokenness.
When you are meek, you understand surrender.
When you pursue righteousness, you understand *dependence*.

The Christian life is a life of dependence, yet by our very nature we are often *stubbornly independent,* and this independence leaves us always striving but never feeling filled. Righteousness is being in right standing with God. To be hungry and thirsty for righteousness means being desperate to stay in step with God and to live in His presence.

After my dog Jake spent a week with a great trainer, I sensed another change in him. He discovered the joy of pleasing his master. In spiritual terms, Jake was hungry and thirsty for righteousness.

He was desperate to stay by my side.

When I moved, he moved.

When I stopped, he stopped.

If I told him to stay, he would stay.

When I said come, he would come.

When I was in the house, he lay down at my feet.

In the morning, when I got up, he got up too.

At night, when I went to bed, he went to bed.

Jake is desperate to please me, obey me, and stay in step with me. He does all this with his tail wagging. He has discovered the *blessing of obedience* and *living in my presence*. This is exactly how Jesus says we are to relate to God, and this is how he related to the Father.

Jesus stayed in step with his Father, and when we stay in step with our Heavenly Father, when we hunger and thirst for righteousness, God blesses us. When my dog stays in step with me, he has everything he needs and usually gets a couple of treats. All Jake has to do is stay close to me, and he is blessed. All that he needs flows out of our relationship.

Jake lives in complete dependence, and he's *happy*.

We can choose to stay close to our master and be blessed too.

Psalm 37:4 says, "Delight yourself in the Lord, and He will give you the desires of your heart." Psalm 84:11 says, "No good things does He withhold from those who walk upright." In Matthew 6:33, Jesus reminds us to "Seek first the kingdom of God and His righteousness, and all these things shall be added unto you."

In John chapter fifteen, Jesus says, "I am the true vine...He who remains (meaning lives in my presence) in me will bear much fruit, but apart from me you can do nothing." This illustration is a constant reminder that all I need flows from my relationship with Jesus.

That does not mean I can be a lukewarm, casual Christian who loves God at a distance until I need something, and when things go wrong, run over for a handout. Think about if a vine disconnected from its roots until it "needed" something. It wouldn't take long to shrivel up and die. It has to stay connected to be blessed. You and I are no different. When we walk with God, our relationship with God and people flourishes, and all I need for life comes to me as I follow Him.

We are blessed.

I've seen this play out my whole life. It was because I was following Jesus that I dated and married Tina. It's why I attended UNCW and felt called into ministry. It's why Tina and I went to seminary. It's how we survived and grew through our marriage crisis and now have three incredible kids. It's why we are now in a ministry that is growing and reaching a community.

It's important to hear this: everything in your life is the fruit of walking with God *or* walking independently of Him. If I walk with Him, He works in everything for my good (Romans 8:28)! To hunger and thirst for righteousness means I *eagerly desire* to live in God's presence to stay in step with Him.

Often our disappointment and heartache come from our misplaced expectations. Gautama Buddha taught that suffering is eliminated when desire is eliminated. Jesus makes it clear our desire, longings, and appetite is not the problem. The question is *what are you hungry for?*

If we want to be blessed, our hunger and thirst for righteousness must be stronger than our hunger and thirst for the American dream. Our desire to know and walk with God must be greater than our love and desire for this world.

We go to school, build a career, and start a family because of these God-given desires. This is not bad. In fact, you could argue that we are simply fulfilling God's mandate for us to be fruitful and multiply and fill the earth. However, the danger comes when we are so captivated by the world that our appetite for God is greatly diminished. When we become so full of what is good, we can lose our appetite for what is great.

Jesus says if we want to be blessed, we must hunger and thirst for what is great—the person and presence of God. When I look back on my life, it is obvious now that when Jesus is my first pursuit, everything else takes care of itself. I am able to enjoy God's blessings without being enslaved by them. However, if my pursuit of good things causes me to lose my hunger for God, I end up empty, desperate, and in bondage.

If we are hungry for Jesus, he promises we will be filled.

Lessons in Righteousness

Through the years, Tina and I have learned to live this way with each other. This is one of the secrets to a successful marriage. I am constantly aware of what is going on in Tina's life and how I can serve her. As I am writing this, I know later today she has a chiropractic appointment because of the headache that's been bothering her for a couple of days, and so she needs to work from home. I know what we need to do with the kids, what we are planning for dinner tonight, and our plans for the rest of the week.

I am in step with my wife, and she is in step with me.

We are a team.

We are no longer two, but one.

This is what marriage looks like, and we are *eager* to stay in step with one another. This connection produces times of unexpected intimacy, needed strength, and perspective as we navigate the ongoing issues in life. This connection defines all the rest.

This is the kind of relationship Jesus wants with each of us, not because he demands it, but because it makes life better. This is one reason why the primary metaphor the Bible uses to describe our relationship with Christ is marriage (Ephesians 5:22-32). God does not put us on a leash; instead, we are motivated by His love for us and our love for Him. We want to please Him.

When we understand the grace and generosity of God, we long to stay close to Him. All that we need and long for flows through our connection with Him. This connection with Jesus produces unexpected divine moments, provides strength and comfort during our suffering, and provides a kingdom perspective that defines the rest of our lives.

This is the pursuit of righteousness.

I wonder how many years it took Joseph—away from home and in slavery—before he developed a hunger for righteousness. Nothing empties the soul like losing all you have and becoming a slave. It can't have been long before Joseph was hungry for righteousness and longed for God's presence above all else, because that is where he would find peace.

Can you imagine the prayer he prayed, dirty, broken, and in chains?

God, I am a sinful man; I have created a mess, and I want you to be in charge. I am not sure if I will ever be free, or ever see my family again, or ever prove my innocence, but all those things are secondary. What I cannot live without is Your presence.

Joseph knew his pride had been offensive. His sin caused him to lose what mattered most. He longed to see and embrace his mother, father, and even his brothers again. Joseph could see that his plans and dreams had failed. In this place of brokenness, Joseph hungered and thirsted for righteousness.

If God had anything else planned for Joseph's life, He would have to open the doors—literally. Joseph was no longer calling the shots. He was humble, broken, and surrendered. In his cell, when he was alone in his thoughts, Joseph began to hear the still, small voice of God.

At first it was just a passing thought, but before long, his connection with God was so rich, so tangible, it was almost audible. It was in these quiet moments that Joseph fell in love with God. Some days he was so caught up in his conversations with God that he forgot he was a prisoner. Joseph knew he was a son of God, and despite the steel bars that secured his body, he was free!

Joseph's pursuit of righteousness meant he was no longer concerned about his circumstances, status, future, or dreams. What Joseph valued most was his *intimacy with God*, because in it he felt blessed, satisfied, and content. He had nothing but a hunger and thirst for righteousness that kept him filled.

I wonder how many years it took Moses—day after day, night after night, as he watched over those sheep—to develop a hunger for God's presence. As a shepherd, he realized how easy it was for them to lose their way. He saw how weak and vulnerable they were when they were alone, and how desperately they needed his rod and staff.

I wonder when he realized *I am just like these sheep*.

Moses could see his pride and independence. He probably thought about them as he ran away from his life as a prince and into exile. His half-baked plan to defend the Hebrews, his people, was a complete failure and almost got him killed.

He was done making plans.

He'd stick with herding sheep.

Moses was humble, broken, surrendered—and from now on, God was in charge.

I suspect Moses longed for Egypt. He must have missed the people, the good food, the servants attending to his needs, and all the other comforts he was accustomed to. Moses had lost everything, and yet if he was honest, he found something much greater in that wilderness.

He found a friend (Exodus 33:11).

At first, he thought he was going crazy, spending hours having these conversations with himself. Sheep may be good listeners, but they can't talk back. But through the years it became obvious he was not crazy, and he was not talking to sheep; he was talking to the Shepherd. In the wilderness, with nothing to do but watch over a few sheep, God was real and present.

Why would God waste time hanging out in the wilderness talking to a loner, a fugitive, a shepherd? The same reason he talks to you and me—to fill us up and to make Himself known. Eventually, Moses forgot about Egypt and all he lost. He did not wake up longing for a dip in the Nile but for *living* water.

This was the only thing that could quench his thirst.

Peter longed for Jesus, but he could not stop thinking about that night seven weeks ago when he'd denied his Lord. Forgiving yourself is one thing; forgetting is much more difficult. Every morning, as the sun would begin to rise, the rooster would crow, and Peter would be reminded of his failure.

He was not sure how to move on.

Overwhelmed with guilt, shame, and regret, he must have felt like a failure.

All that big talk and only to become a shell of who he was.

Peter spent much of his time in silence, not sure if he should speak at all. I suspect there came a moment when Peter got down on his knees, heart pounding, tears running down his face, and searching for words to show how he felt. With his face in the dirt, he began to pour out his heart.

I am such a proud man. I have disgraced myself and hurt you. I have made such a mess of things. Jesus, I am so tired of being in charge. I am not sure what to do next. I just want to be with you. Your presence is greater than life. I'm empty. Fill me up.

Peter was desperate for Jesus, and in that desperation, Peter came to a place where he was no longer ashamed. The joy and treasure of remaining in God's presence were far greater than the pleasures of this world (1 Peter 5:12-14). The presence of Christ was his greatest pursuit and treasure.

Everything else was optional. Peter discovered the blessing of living in dependence.

Paul had worked for years to please God. He built his resume and established himself as an emerging leader among the Pharisees. He put in the long hours, the travel from town to town, and was willing to do what most people wouldn't. This included not seeking a wife or beginning a family. It included being tough on crime, violently so.

Paul arrested, tortured, and even put to death Christians all over the Roman empire.

This was more difficult than you might imagine; after all, when these Christians were attacked, they did not fight back; they would just look at Paul and his companions with compassion and would actually pray for them.

Paul hated that more than anything. He could still see their faces and hear their prayers. However, he was convinced the end justified the means. He had to stop these Jesus followers in order to protect the faith.

And then the Damascus road changed his life.

As Paul sat in the darkness, he could see the face of Jesus and was trying to come to grips with his error. He thought he was working for God, but he was working against Him. When Jesus asked with a broken heart, *Why are you persecuting me?* It was almost more than Paul could bear.

There must have come a moment when Paul got on his knees and prayed like this:

God, what have I done? I am so sorry. I have been so prideful and so blind. I have hurt so many people, your people. Please forgive me. I am terrified of making another foolish decision. Just a few days ago I was so sure I was working for you, and now, in the darkness, I can see I was working against you. I am brokenhearted over all the pain I have caused and afraid of being in change. Jesus, take the lead. I am desperate for your presence.

It was dark now, but Paul was discovering the brightening blessing of dependence.

This is where God wants to bring us all—to a place of willful dependence.

However, this can only happen when we put aside our desires and stubborn independence.

In 1997, I can remember being on my knees, wearing holes in the knees of my jeans. Morning after morning, I prayed just like these men prayed. I confessed my prideful independence. I told God how brokenhearted I was over the mess I had created and the pain I had caused. I admitted that I was completely unsure of what to do next. I admitted that I desperately needed God's help because I was afraid to make decisions. I was afraid of making things worse, and I was desperate for God's presence. I was humble, broken, surrendered, and learning dependence.

Then, one day, the emptiness of my spirit was filled with the fullness of His grace.

In my hunger and thirst for God's righteousness, His spirit had filled me up.

And in that moment, I knew there was no turning back.

CHAPTER FIVE

The Merciful

Blessed are the merciful, for they will be shown mercy.

M ercy. It sounds like an old-fashioned word, and in a sense, it is. But mercy is one of the most impactful actions in the world, and it seems like it's needed now more than ever.

I love this definition of mercy: *compassion or forgiveness shown toward someone whom it is within one's power to punish or harm.* We live in a world that's quick to punish, slow to forgive, and almost impossible to forget.

That's why mercy is like a refreshing rainstorm that chases away the heat of a summer day.

There is no one more merciful than the one who invented the word and proved it with His love. God has been so merciful to me.

His mercy for me has taken root and is growing in my heart. That is what fruit does. It has the power to reproduce. God *is* mercy, and when His mercy is growing in my life, it empowers me to show mercy to others.

When we understand the gospel, the mercy and generosity of God toward sinners, it produces mercy in our lives. Let me say it bluntly: if you have a problem showing mercy to others, you have never experienced mercy yourself. You are not poor in Spirit, because those who are poor in spirit have experienced God's mercy.

If we are not careful, religion will teach us to *act* merciful, without going through the first four steps of humility, brokenness, surrender, and dependence. Without adjusting our posture towards God, our act of mercy towards others is merely self-serving. Religious people only act mercifully when it benefits them. When God's mercy is present, it is often a surprise; it is unexpected and offered to those who do not deserve it—even, perhaps especially—when we have nothing to gain.

Religion produces a very different kind of character than that of a relationship with Christ.

One of the most unfortunate effects of religion is that religion makes people proud and judgmental. Rather than humble dependence that arises from a proper understanding of our spiritual condition apart from Christ and experiencing the transforming power of God's grace, religious people are prideful and independent. They have been trained to follow the rules, to manage their public image, and to know the right answers, and they do these things well.

But they do not understand how to walk with God or people.

They believe their standing with God is based on their performance rather than the work of Christ. Religion makes people insensitive, uncaring, and mean-spirited—the opposite of merciful. Just look on Facebook. The religious people (and I'm using *religion* in the broadest sense) on both sides of the political aisle constantly reveal the fruit of their hearts. They expose themselves and are blinded by their pride.

It's difficult sometimes, but I have mercy for them.

And this has come through years of hard-won experience.

Lessons in Mercy

The first church I pastored was in a small rural town in eastern North Carolina.

I was young and inexperienced, but even I could sense God doing some pretty amazing stuff. In the first year, the church grew from a weekly attendance of 65 on a Sunday morning to almost 200. Forty-eight people were saved and baptized that year. In a 100-year-old church located in a town of 1,500, this was revival!

However, revival is hard work, even when God's doing most of the heavy lifting.

I was preaching and teaching four times a week and attending seminary full time. Tina was in college full time, and we were both commuting an hour or more to school. Plus, we were still trying to rebuild our young marriage.

The truth is, there was more to do than I could do, so I was forced to decide where to spend my time. The church also had lots of senior adults. We had eighteen senior adult shut-ins who were accustomed to getting a visit from the pastor every couple of weeks. Although I enjoyed visiting with them, I just could not keep up. I encouraged the deacons and other church leaders to help but did not get any response. This caused some to question my love for the senior adults.

The problem was not my heart but my schedule.

Then I made two leadership decisions that sent everyone over the edge. From the church's small budget, I bought fifty Bibles, without asking, for all the people we had just baptized. The Bibles were not expensive, and we had plenty of money in the bank, but I was too inexperienced to know I needed to ask for permission before buying Bibles.

About that time, I also found out an important and very visible leader in the church was having a very public and visible affair. In a small town, everyone knows your business. I asked the leader to step down and offered to help the couple rebuild their marriage. After what Tina and I had been through, helping struggling couples had become something we were both passionate about and good at. Instead, the leader and her family got mad at me for removing her from her position.

This was my first church. I was doing my best but was in over my head. The emotion over these three issues converged and seemed to feed on one another, so I asked a local denominational leader to help.

After I explained what was happening, he believed we needed to have a church-wide meeting to talk about the concerns people had. The purpose of the meeting was to give everyone a chance to talk about their concerns and be heard. Then we could provide answers and come up with a plan for moving forward.

I was actually looking forward to the meeting because I thought it would get everything out in the open and help the church to understand my heart behind the decisions I made and how those decisions benefited the church. When I arrived, the church was packed. That should have alerted me to the trouble that was ahead, but I was actually encouraged that so many people cared enough to show up and talk.

This was going to be a great meeting!

When the meeting started, I knew something was wrong when the first person who stood to speak was someone I did not know and had never seen. Who was this guy, and why was he at "our" meeting? It turns out he was a relative of the dismissed leader and a church "member." That night, I met lots of church "members" who I had never seen before.

For almost two hours, person after person expressed their anger and hatred toward me while the church members who knew and loved me sat silently in shock. I could never figure out what they were mad about. I was working my tail off. The church was growing like never before. I bought Bibles for new believers, I offered to help with a marriage in crisis, and these people I loved so much seemed to think I was the devil.

It was a painful and eye-opening night for Tina and me.

They showed no mercy. Like sharks who smell blood in the water, they were in a frenzy.

Sadly and ironically, it is often hard to find mercy in church.

What causes this? A lack of mercy is a sure sign of a religious culture, and many churches are filled with "religious" people. They know the rules but lack a dynamic relationship with God. When people lack mercy, it is because they have never experienced mercy. They are so proud and self-righteous that they do not see their need for God's mercy. They think God *owes them* for being so good at following the rules.

Just like the religious community and leaders that Jesus was speaking to, most people have a heart problem. That's why the first four Beatitudes deal with the heart and look inward. If we do not let Jesus transform our hearts, we can never build the capacity to love and serve each other. If we do not allow Jesus to work on our hearts, even what appears to be good is usually motivated by our own self-interest. If we have not taken the first four steps of humility, brokenness, surrender, and dependence, over time, church can make us worse, not better.

Unfortunately, church often teaches us to follow rules, manage our image, and choose political alliances rather than how to cultivate a transformational relationship with Jesus.

Only Jesus can produce mercy.

Religion makes the church a pride-filled, judgmental, no mercy zone.

Yet, Jesus was full of mercy!

In John chapter 8, Jesus is teaching in the temple when the religious leaders drag a woman before him who had been caught in the act of adultery. These religious leaders said to Jesus, "The law says to stone her to death; what do you say?"

They were trying to trap Jesus and were willing to sacrifice this woman to do it. It was the original *cancel culture.* They outed her and publicly shamed her, but that wasn't enough. Now they wanted to end her life. They were hoping Jesus would either deny the authority of the law (something they knew he wouldn't do) or stone the woman to death for her sins.

Either way, they would successfully damage his reputation and influence with the Jewish community. Instead, Jesus knelt down and began writing in the dust. Can you imagine their surprise? Jesus never did what people expected, so when Jesus stood back up, his words were quiet but powerful: *Let the one who has never sinned throw the first stone.*

I can imagine the stones as big as fists falling one by one to the ground as these "religious" leaders thought about the implications for their own sin-filled lives. They would never have wanted their sins brought forth for the world to see.

The point Jesus was making is that we are all sinners, and we have all been shown mercy. Since this is true, we should be merciful to others. The religious leaders were unaware of their need for mercy, but they were good at protecting their reputation. They were good at keeping the law and judgmental toward everyone else.

What Jesus is trying to help us understand is this: because you have received mercy, offer it freely to others. It's a powerful thought. We have freely received mercy, so let's not charge others for it. This woman was not the only person Jesus was trying to save that day. She needed mercy for her sexual sin, and the religious leaders needed mercy for their pride.

Two thousand years later, the impact of that lesson still holds true.

One of the reasons Jesus is so merciful is because he has walked in our shoes. I love what Hebrews 4:15-16 says, "For we do not have a high priest who is unable to empathize with our weaknesses, but we have one who has been tempted in every way, just as we are—yet he did not sin. Let us then approach God's throne of grace with confidence, so that we may receive MERCY and find grace to help us in our time of need."

James, the half-brother of Jesus, says in James 2:13, "Judgment without mercy will be shown to anyone who has not been merciful. Mercy triumphs over judgment." Jesus was merciful to James and Jude, his brothers, after the resurrection when they finally believed. In Matthew 9:13 Jesus says, "But go and learn what this means: 'I desire mercy, not sacrifice.' For I have not come to call the righteous, but sinners."

Religious people are proud of their sacrifices, their works, what they think they know, and what they can do. But those who have come face-to-face with Jesus become *aware* of their sinfulness and are overwhelmed by his mercy. Such people show mercy to others. The prophet Micah said, "Do justice, love mercy, and walk humbly with your God." (Micah 6:8)

America has lost its mercy.

Today everyone seems to be attacking everyone. American culture is religious, proud, angry, judgmental, and increasingly violent. For the last 70 years, America has intentionally evicted God. We have raised children to believe that people are an accident rather than God's special creation. We have raised children on positive self-esteem, convincing them that they are the center of the universe. We have rejected moral absolutes and are surprised when everyone does what is right in their own eyes. This makes it almost impossible for people today to see that they are spiritually bankrupt.

How can you mourn over sin when you do not even believe in sin?

How can you be meek when you have been told your entire life how special you are?

Our hunger and thirst for righteousness is nonexistent because we are so full of *good* things that we have no room for the *great*. It's no wonder we have a world without mercy.

America is in crisis.

Not only are we dealing with a global pandemic, racial division, political division, and a financial recession, but we have lost our ability to *talk* about what we are going through. Rather than talking and discovering our similarities, everyone is attacking the "bad guys" on the other side.

Why is it so hard for us to show mercy and compassion to people who are hurting? Because we have not taken the first four steps Jesus lays out in the Sermon on the Mount, and it is destroying the blessing he wants to give us.

It's as simple as this—*every* person in your life needs mercy from time to time.

It's time to stop shooting the wounded, canceling the imperfect, and casting stones when people fall short of our expectations. That's not mercy, and that will never lead to blessing.

The next time you feel the need to punish or pass judgment on someone, think about how God has treated you. When you experience His mercy firsthand, you can't help but share it with others.

CHAPTER SIX

The Pure in Heart

Blessed are the pure in heart, for they will see God.

D o you ever wonder if people get tired of faking it? I do.
It seems like in this social media-enhanced world we live in, it's impossible to get a glimpse of who someone really is. Photoshopped and filtered pictures show the perfect family on a perfect vacation eating perfect meals and always getting along.

It's exhausting to have to be something or someone you are not.

This is why Jesus spoke the sixth Beatitude—*blessed are the pure in heart.*

Of course, they didn't have social media back then, but Jesus knew that human nature is always to pretend to be something you aren't—after all, we've been doing it since Adam and Eve covered themselves in the Garden of Eden.

What does it mean to be "pure in heart?"

The best modern word would be authenticity. It carries with it the idea of being sincere, free of deceit, hypocrisy, or falseness. Someone who is pure in heart is an honest, unadulterated person of integrity.

Pure in heart *does not* mean without fault, sinless, or perfect. But it does mean you are real. In the Old Testament, David is a classic example of a pure heart. In fact, the Bible says he is a man after God's own heart (1 Samuel 13:14). David certainly was not perfect (all you have to do is read his story to see that), but he was sincere. He was not a person of pretense. I believe when you were with David, what you saw is what you got.

God saw this too and chose him to be king.

Lessons in Purity

Jesus says the pure in heart will see God.

Why is authenticity so important to God?

Because God hates hypocrisy!

Just read Matthew 23 and see how Jesus confronts the lack of integrity and sincerity and the abundance of hypocrisy of the religious leaders. Hypocrisy is an expression of pride and independence. It is a person's attempt to exalt themselves in the eyes of others and steal God's glory.

This is the sin of Satan.

Satan is full of pride and wants to steal God's glory (Isaiah 14:12-15), but God will not share His glory with anyone (Isaiah 42:8). Hypocrisy is an attempt to elevate myself and appear righteous through my own efforts. It is when we want people to be impressed with us rather than God (Matthew 23:5-7).

Jesus wants the opposite from us. He wants us to humble ourselves and point people to him. This is one reason John the Baptist was so effective. He did not exalt himself and gather people to himself (even though he could have). Unlike the religious leaders, John understood his job was to point people to Jesus (John 3:26-30).

It may be helpful here to step back a moment and think about what purity looks like. Do you remember seeing those commercials where the infomercial host would have a jar of dirty water sitting next to a jar of clean water? He'd grab his bottle of magic cleaner and give the dirty water a squirt. Presto! Changeo! The dirty water would become clean.

But here's an important question: would you drink the (formerly) dirty water?

Probably not, because all that gunk that was in there before is still in there. It just *looks* clean on the outside, but the inside is still unfit to drink. This is how it is with hypocrisy. The outside looks good, but the inside is a mess.

It's even worse than that though, because it blocks you from seeing God.

Hypocrisy is an attempt to find your identity and validation from people by exalting yourself over others. However, hypocrisy is a lie. It is dishonest and usually abusive. Hypocrisy says, *I'm good—better than you—because of my good works.* Hypocrisy places a religious burden on the backs of others that no one can carry. Jesus says it this way: "They crush people with unbearable religious demands and never lift a finger to ease the burden" (Matthew 23:4).

Jesus came to lighten our burden (Matthew 11:30, 1 John 5:3), and he does so when we pursue him with a pure heart. This is one reason why Jesus reduced all the law down to two life-giving commands: "Love God, and Love your neighbor as yourself" (Matthew 22:38-39).

Just think how different the world would be if we did just those two things.

Jesus wants us to humble ourselves, have mercy for those who are struggling, kneel down, and help them up. That is what Jesus did for us (John 13:1-17)! Jesus wants us to point people to him (Matthew 5:13-16). As we point people to Jesus and help them find life in Christ, we can't help but look good. However, we will always be like the moon. No matter how full or how large, the moon only reflects the light of the sun. It cannot produce light on its own.

We are to reflect the light of the Son to a hurting world. When we understand this, our hearts are purified. We become authentic, and that fuels our transformation.

The other problem with hypocrisy is that it robs us of healing because of what it does to love. Love heals, so where there is love, healing naturally occurs. Hypocrisy keeps us from healing, because it keeps us from love. Here's why. If I am a hypocrite and you love "me", you do not actually love the *real* me because I've kept that person hidden from you. You actually love my false self. In my hypocrisy, you can only love my performance. You may not even know I am a hypocrite.

However, I know it, and because I know I'm faking, there can never be intimacy between us.

The reason people put on an act is because they do not believe God or other people would love them if they were authentic. Therefore, they carefully manage their image to secure love. It's like only being willing to take a posed photo that focuses on your "good side".

The problem is that this is a perpetuating cycle.

Rather than providing me love and producing healing, this shields me from love and becomes another wound. I can see you love my performance, therefore you must not love the real me, so I do more of the things that you love and fall farther and farther from my authentic self—the person God made me to be.

The only way to heal is to come out of hiding, stop pretending, and let people get to know the real you. Jesus says the pure in heart, those who live an authentic life and experience God's love, experience healing. They experience God.

Many church people are stuck in their pain because they have been afraid to be authentic. They are afraid of being rejected, and so they manage their image with precision and care. No hair is out of place; no vulnerability is shared. They are shallow shells of all they could be. They come to church faithfully but never learn to spend time one-on-one with God.

They agree murder is wrong but hate people who are different or disagree with their politics.

They are against adultery but privately look at porn.

They are angry that prayer was removed from school yet they do not pray.

You would never know this about them by looking at them. They carefully manage their image, but all this hiding is robbing them of love and healing and keeps them isolated and alone.

It's only when you take off your mask and come out of hiding that you can experience the healing power of God's love.

Hypocrisy stunts our spiritual growth because we can start to believe the lie we've created. We block God from working to change our character. We attempt to convince people that we are better than we are while hiding our secret sins and the true condition of our hearts.

This hiding keeps us from growing and changing.

It keeps us from seeing God.

Everyone must decide whether to manage their image or allow God to transform their character. You cannot do both. Character change requires humble dependence on God and purity of heart.

When you allow God to do His work, as God transforms your character, you can be honest and transparent about your journey, give God all the glory, invite others to follow Jesus, and experience that same kind of transformation. It's a powerful testimony.

When this happens in the church, the children of God become a breath of fresh air. The church becomes a place of healing and transformation. The children of God are known for their love, humility, joy, peace, and strength. This is something our world desperately needs.

This is why Jesus wants to produce in us a pure heart, a heart of authenticity.

Unfortunately, for many, the pride and hypocrisy of the church have been stumbling blocks. But the church should be an authentic people, the pure in heart, who are being transformed by His grace and helping other people experience and be transformed by this grace. Authenticity is born out of our experience with Jesus.

If we understand the first four Beatitudes, then there is no reason to fake it.

If we do not understand the first four Beatitudes, we can't help but fake it.

You can either change or fake it, but you cannot do both. When you are humbled, broken, surrendered, and sensitive to God's presence, you cannot help but be pure in heart, authentic. When you are prideful, entitled, controlling, and independent, you cannot help but live in hypocrisy.

When Tina and I went through our crisis, I began to see my hypocrisy up close and personally. It's not that I didn't mean well. If you met me, you may have concluded that I was one of the leading students on campus, and you would have been right. From all outward appearances, that is what I seemed to be. I wanted to please God, but I did not know how to follow Jesus yet. I was following the rules publicly, but I did not understand the Beatitudes internally.

I was a hypocrite.

I was managing my image, trying to impress others, but my life was a mess. When I met Dr. Bennett, that began to change. I was a seminary dropout with a failing marriage, so there was no need to pretend anymore. I was very honest about the condition of my soul and marriage. Dr. Bennett was merciful, and he began to show me how to walk with God.

As I learned to live in humble dependence, my character began to change, and it became very natural to be authentic. I had nothing to hide and nothing to prove. Jesus was changing my life, and I wanted everyone to have that same experience with him.

Jesus says the pure in heart will see God, and I could see Him clearly for the first time.

As I learned to spend time with Jesus, I could see, very clearly, that he was changing my life. I could see God. I was learning that without Jesus, despite my best efforts, I was spiritually bankrupt. I was mourning the condition of my soul, the loss of my ministry, and the pain Tina was experiencing. I could see my pride and independence and how it was destroying my life.

I wanted to follow Jesus.

I was glad for Jesus to be in charge.

I was discovering the joy and delight of his presence.

Purity of heart is a goal worth pursuing. It's exhausting to try and be something and someone you are not. Ultimately, it's all going to come out in the end anyway. If you want to truly see God, it's time to redefine who you are and be authentically you. It's the only way to be blessed and the only way to be happy.

CHAPTER SEVEN

The Peacemakers

Blessed are the peacemakers, for they
will be called children of God.

Y ou can learn a lot about people by observing their driving habits. For example, if you were ever to ride with me, this is what you would learn—I am *always* in a hurry. I don't mean to be; it's just that no matter where I am going, I want to be there yesterday. I am impatient. I am an activator. I want to move.

That's not all you'd learn though.

Because I want to get there yesterday, I am always scanning the traffic and looking for any way possible to speed up my arrival time. This is how I approach most things in life. I'm always looking to see if there is a better way, a quicker way, or a more enjoyable way to do things.

But I work hard to make sure this doesn't come at the expense of others.

It's amazing how easy it is for people to lose their cool behind the wheel. If someone pulls in front of me and slows me down, it may cost me a few seconds, but is that worth getting in a fight over?

Twenty-five years ago, I met one guy who thought so.

I was living in Wilmington, North Carolina at the time and was on my way home from the beach. It was a two-lane highway, and I had just slid left over the dashed line to pass a slower driver. At the same time, a car came rushing up behind me and was tailgating me like we were driving on a Nascar track. As soon as I passed the car on my right, I pulled back over into the right lane, so the car on my bumper could go by. He was apparently in an even bigger hurry than I was. As he passed me on the left, I looked over at him, and he casually flipped me off.

I just smiled and sarcastically waved as he drove by.

Apparently, this was the wrong thing to do; his next actions showed he did not like that. He immediately pulled in front of me and began slowing down, and he kept slowing down until he came to a complete stop. The traffic behind me all stopped and I was stuck. I could not go around, back up, or go anywhere. Things escalated a little more when he got out of his car and started walking back to where I was stuck.

He approached my door and began screaming at me and pounding on the window.

At that moment, I had a choice. I could escalate the situation, or I could be a peacemaker.

With a great deal of self-control, I chose the latter.

He ran himself out of steam, got back in the car, and the incident was over. I hope that never happens again, but every time I look back on that moment, it's a reminder of how angry people can get today over things that do not seem to matter.

There are plenty of things in this world we should be mad about; traffic is not one of them.

That's why the world needs peacemakers.

Lessons in Peacemaking

It's no surprise, but Jesus was a peacemaker.

So much so that he gave up his life to create peace between us and the Father.

However, this does not mean Jesus was a wimp.

Jesus was not weak or passive. In fact, there are a handful of times when Jesus lost his cool and let people have it. Why would Jesus get angry? Jesus does not get angry when people mistreat him. (There are no recorded incidents of Jesus riding his donkey too slowly and getting into a screaming match with the person riding his...*tail.*)

Jesus saved his anger for more justified reasons. He got angry when religious people—who should know better—mistreated others and became a barrier between people and God (Matthew 21:12-13, Matthew 23:13-14). Jesus came to be a bridge. He wants us to be a bridge, not a barrier, so everyone has an opportunity to experience a blessed life.

This is why peacemaking is so important.

When we get offended, it's usually because we are not getting our way. James says our conflict is caused by wanting our way and being willing to scheme and even kill to get it (James 4). James, like Jesus, wants us to fight *for* people, not *with* them.

That's what a peacemaker does.

Peacemakers understand that the relationship is more important than anything we are fighting over. They are more interested in brokering peace than being right.

Think about the last time you were angry about something.

What were you angry about? Were you angry because you were not getting your way, or were you angry over the injustice, suffering, or pain you see in our world? That's the difference between selfish anger and righteous anger.

Jesus recognized that peacemakers are blessed and will be called children of God because they focused more on their similarities than their differences. Peacemakers stand together and work for peace.

As I'm writing the draft of this chapter, this week our nation once again witnessed the senseless murder of an innocent black man, and protests have started all over the country. Like countless others, I watched the video of George Floyd being murdered, and it broke my heart. I am gutted over the pain and division this act has caused and the wound that continues to fester.

I am also angry that it keeps happening.

I am angry that the black men I know live in constant fear that they or their sons could be next. However, I cannot allow my anger to get the best of me. I am never justified in attacking someone else physically or verbally to settle the score.

In the midst of pain, division, and despair, God has called us to be peacemakers.

But how do we do that when it is so easy to give in to the anger?

Jesus modeled this perfectly in Mark 12. One day some religious leaders approached Jesus. They were politically connected to Herod, the evil and cruel tetrarch who ruled Galilee. Their goal was simple—trap Jesus in a way that would offend Herod and the other rulers.

The execution, however, wasn't so simple, because Jesus saw right through them.

The Jewish people were being abused and oppressed by Rome. Their religious leaders, who should have been fighting for their people, were instead religious hypocrites and traitors. They were being paid by Rome to control the Jews. Rather than being spiritual leaders, they became political leaders.

So when they approached Jesus that day and asked him, "Should we pay taxes?" they thought the trap was set. Rather than engage them in a debate, Jesus simply asked for a Roman coin. Jesus always had a way of doing the unexpected, and this time would be no different.

Coin in hand, Jesus asked them whose picture and title were stamped in the metal.

Of course, the image and name was Caesar.

Jesus's answer: "Give to Caesar what belongs to Caesar, and give to God what belongs to God" (Mark 12:13-17). Jesus did not allow politics to hijack his ministry. (That's a lesson a lot of Christians could learn these days.) He would not allow their immaturity to bait him into a fight or force him into picking sides.

Instead, he wanted us to understand the real issue.

His mission was bigger, and his calling was higher.

The real issue was not who owned the money but who owns your heart. And that is still the issue. If we settle the ownership of our hearts, our political questions turn out to be not that complicated.

And yet, even in the body of Christ, there is always the need to be a peacemaker.

I received an email from a friend this week. He was upset about the message I preached last Sunday. In it, I pointed out and condemned the racial injustice I see in our nation. The letter was pretty aggressive, and as I read his email, something interesting happened. I was reading words, and my mind was saying *you should be offended; you need to give him a piece of your mind*, but my heart was saying *be a peacemaker*.

So I called him up and pursued a conversation. We talked, we cried, we shared our frustrations, our pain, and our fears. We affirmed our love and support for each other and prayed together before ending the call.

If I'm being honest, I was surprised by my response.

There was a time in my life when I was angry and defensive. I took everything so personally. An email like that one would have sent me over the edge. But as I look back, I am humbled and amazed that God has set me free from anger and insecurity. I am encouraged to see my growing freedom from the approval of people. I was able to listen—without agreeing or disagreeing—with an open heart and bring peace into his pain.

That is what peacemakers do.

Not because it is a rule, but because with Christ's help, that is who we are.

This week my daughter went to Starbucks because like most teenagers, she thinks buying burnt coffee from Starbucks is cool. But I digress. When she turned into the parking lot, it appeared a lady in front of her was pulling into a parking space, so she drove around her car and headed for the drive-through.

Unfortunately, my daughter was wrong.

The lady was on her way to the drive-through, and my daughter had inadvertently skipped her in line. The lady was irate. My daughter could see her mouthing stuff and waving her arms around in obvious frustration. She felt bad, but what could she do? She was in line, boxed in, with cars on every side.

When she approached the window the Holy Spirit whispered, *Buy her coffee.*

Abby paid for her own drink *and* the drink of the angry lady behind her. In that moment, she was a peacemaker, and I am one proud dad! At seventeen years old, that would have been the last thing I would have thought of.

The truth is, being a peacemaker is not natural, but *supernatural.* It is not something we work up, but something God produces in us as our relationship with Him grows. We see it time and again in the Bible.

Abraham was a peacemaker. In Genesis 13, Abram (later renamed Abraham), Lot, and their families had been living and traveling together. However, both families had grown very large and the land was unable to support them all. Their herdsmen were beginning to fight over who had rights to land and water. In the middle of this conflict, Abram said to Lot, "Let's not allow this conflict to come between us or our herdsmen. After all, we are close relatives. The whole country is open to you. Take your choice of any section of the land you want, and we will separate. If you want the land to the left, then I'll take the land to the right. If you prefer the land on the right, then I'll go to the left."

This is the sign of a peacemaker!

Abram was Lot's uncle, and as his elder would certainly have been justified in demanding the best of the land. However, Abram knew God had promised to bless him. With this in mind, he valued his relationship with Lot and Lot's family over any piece of land.

Peter did not start out as a peacemaker. He was proud, independent, and strong.

Like most religious people, Peter probably had a difficult time seeing his need for God. He may have even felt like he was doing

Jesus a favor. When Peter said, "Even if everyone else deserts you, I'll stay and even die for you." Peter had not learned humble dependence. Peter had not experienced his crisis moment yet.

In the garden when Jesus was arrested, Peter pulled out his sword and was ready to fight!

That may have been brave, but it did little to broker peace.

What Peter did not recognize in that moment was that he had become a barrier rather than a bridge. His violence would only confirm what many believed—Jesus was an imposter with a political agenda.

After Jesus was arrested, and Peter's denial, he reached the point of mourning, brokenness, surrender and dependence. He was done leading and ready to follow, so he headed back to the place where Jesus invited him to follow (John 21:3).

He didn't know what he'd find there, only that he was desperate to please Jesus (John 21:17).

He is ready to be a bridge-builder and in Acts, we see where Peter, the rough and tumble Galilean fisherman becomes a peacemaker. He pours out his heart in a very authentic way to a crowd of people. He holds nothing back and tells the crowd about Jesus while putting the religious leaders on notice. *I may be a peacemaker, but I'm also a truth-teller, and nothing and no one is going to stop me from preaching the good news of Jesus Christ.* That day, over 3000 people were saved, and Peter the stumbling block became Peter the bridge- builder. He had become a peacemaker.

Peace is powerful.

Blessed are the peacemakers.

CHAPTER EIGHT

The Persecuted

Blessed are those who are persecuted
because of righteousness, for theirs
is the kingdom of heaven.

J esus saved the best (or perhaps the most puzzling) "blessed" statement for last.

Chances are, if you had met Jesus, the man, when he was ministering in the first century, you would have liked him. It's my guess that almost everyone did. As a person, he was kind, loving, gentle, and direct. He spoke the truth but without the malice that seems to accompany truth today.

He healed the sick and cast out demons.

Crowds clamored just to be near him, to catch a glimpse of him at work.

I think Jesus had a sense of humor and a streak of mischievousness. He probably made his disciples laugh and was fun to be around. That was Jesus the man.

But he was also the Son of God, and this is where the problems began.

The Sermon on the Mount marked the beginning of his public ministry, and right out of the gate Jesus warns everyone—*following me will cost you something.* The Jews in the first century assumed that when the Messiah arrived the battle would be over. They pictured a Messiah who would free them from Roman oppression and usher in an unprecedented time of peace and prosperity.

Jesus came to free *all* humanity from *spiritual* oppression and usher in his kingdom.

However, he refused to allow his kingdom ministry to be hijacked by their political agenda.

So when the secular brushes up against the sacred, sparks are bound to fly.

That's why Jesus warns us that when we follow him we will face persecution.

Sometimes in America today we give people the impression that following Jesus leads to a life of health, wealth, and prosperity. Then when people begin to follow Jesus and have a different experience, they reject Jesus and the Christian faith. It feels to them like a bait-and-switch.

But Jesus never promised us an easy life of prosperity.

Jesus did invite us into a life of blessing, but that blessing is not dependent on our circumstances. The blessing comes from a strong relationship with God and each other. Jesus said, "In this world you will have trouble. But take heart! I have overcome the world" (John 16:33). "If the world hates you, remember that it hated me first. The world would love you as one of its own if you belonged to it, but you are no longer part of the world. I chose you to come out of the world, so it hates you. Do you remember what I told you? 'A slave is not greater than the master.' Since they persecuted me, naturally they will persecute you" (John 15:18-20). "You will be arrested, persecuted, and killed. You will be hated all over the world because you are my followers" (Matthew 24:9).

Sounds like fun, doesn't it?

Following him, at times, would be painful.

So why did the disciples do it?

The best answer comes from Peter when Jesus asks the disciples if they want to walk away from him. "*Simon Peter answered him, 'Lord, to whom shall we go? You have the words of eternal life. We have come to believe and to know that you are the Holy One of God'*" (John 6:68-69).

When the secular sees the sacred, everything else fades, and no cost is too high a price.

So the disciples who stuck with Jesus all experienced the truth of this persecution personally. Peter was crucified upside down. Paul was beheaded. Andrew was crucified. Thomas was pierced through with four spears. Phillip was crucified. Matthew was stabbed to death. Bartholomew was crucified. James was stoned and clubbed to death. Simon the Zealot burned alive. Matthias was burned to death. John was boiled alive in oil but supernaturally protected and then banished to the Island of Patmos where he wrote five New Testament books.

Were the disciples blessed? Yes!

The blessing comes through the fulfillment of the promise. The humble have ownership in the kingdom of heaven. Those who mourn are comforted. The meek will inherit the earth. Those who are dependent will be satisfied. The merciful will receive mercy. The authentic will see God. The peacemakers will be called the children of God.

When we are persecuted, we can rejoice, because great is our reward in heaven.

This means we must learn to live with an eternal perspective.

Lessons in Perspective

In America, most Christians will never suffer physically for their faith. However, in the years to come, I believe it is going to be increasingly difficult to follow Christ. Recently a church in Mississippi was burned down for not obeying the governor's orders and conducting church services during the pandemic. A prominent church in Alabama was thrown out of two high schools, forced to close a community center that serves the poor, its members banned from serving the poor with the housing authority, and accused of racism because the pastor liked a Facebook post supporting the 'wrong" political party.

Just this week an outspoken activist for a large, radical, politically-motivated, social justice organization accused churches of racism and said they are a symbol of white supremacy and should be vandalized.

The Bible and the teaching of Jesus will never be politically correct. Paul warned us in 2 Timothy 3-4, that in the last days people would turn away from the truth and Christians would face persecution. This persecution comes from both inside and outside the church. I believe the American church, in the years to come, will experience an increased pressure to compromise the truth and increased persecution for refusing to do so.

When Christians are insulted, slandered, and lied about, Jesus says rejoice! He says stay strong, steadfast, and unshakeable. Live with an eternal perspective, and look forward to the great reward coming.

One of the most difficult aspects of ministry is doing what is right and being attacked for it. This has happened countless times throughout the years. Once, in my first church, we did a community outreach. I was still in seminary, and about 50 of my seminary buddies came to help. We divided into teams of three, one trained seminary student paired up with two church members. Each team was given a map of the area and assigned a group of houses to visit.

It seemed like a powerful way to reach the community.

When the chairman of the deacons and I were planning all this, we rode around town (it was a small town of only 1,500) counting houses and making maps. As I drove down the street, he counted out loud. "One, two, colored house, three, colored house, colored house."

I interrupted and asked, "Why are you not counting all the houses?" His response broke my heart: "Because colored people live there." I told him to count every house because we would be visiting all of them, and that these families would be welcome in our church. As you can imagine, quite a few people were upset about this. However, as a pastor, I have to do what is right even when people do not like it, do not understand it, or do not agree with it.

At the end of the day, I have decided to live to please Jesus, not people.

When Tina and I were going through our marriage crisis, there were many days when I wondered—is this going to work? Am I getting through? Is Tina going to come around? Am I making a difference? In those moments, God reminded me that one day I would stand before Him and give an account for my life. I would answer for how I loved Tina. I would not answer for Tina's response. I decided I would love her even if she never loved me back, even if she left, and even if our marriage never recovered. I would live to please

Jesus and trust him with the rest. Jesus says when we live this way, there is a great reward coming!

Paul lived this way. He experienced incredible suffering for the gospel. In 2 Corinthians 11:23-28 Paul said wrote this:

Are they servants of Christ? I know I sound like a madman, but I have served him far more! I have worked harder, been put in prison more often, been whipped times without number, and faced death again and again. Five different times the Jewish leaders gave me thirty-nine lashes. Three times I was beaten with rods. Once I was stoned. Three times I was shipwrecked. Once I spent a whole night and a day adrift at sea. I have traveled on many long journeys. I have faced danger from rivers and from robbers. I have faced danger from my own people, the Jews, as well as from the Gentiles. I have faced danger in the cities, in the deserts, and on the seas. And I have faced danger from men who claim to be believers but are not. I have worked hard and long, enduring many sleepless nights. I have been hungry and thirsty and have often gone without food. I have shivered in the cold, without enough clothing to keep me warm. Then, besides all this, I have the daily burden of my concern for all the churches.

I cannot even imagine going through this, and yet Paul says about his suffering, "For our present troubles are small and won't last very long. Yet they produce for us a glory that vastly outweighs them and will last forever! So, we don't look at the troubles we can see now; rather, we fix our gaze on things that cannot be seen. For the things we see now will soon be gone, but the things we cannot see will last forever" (2 Corinthians 4:17-18).

Paul understood that his suffering for the gospel was producing a great reward. He'd come face-to-face with the sacred on the road to Damascus, and he knew that pursuing righteousness and sharing the good news of Jesus Christ was all that mattered.

One of the skills of great communicators is to say something that shocks their audience and captures their attention. It gets them thinking about what is coming next. I can picture Jesus using this technique in his Sermon on the Mount.

Jesus climbed to the top of the mountain and found a place to sit.

All the eyes of his disciples and the crowd were on him.

He knew that he needed to get their attention and keep it.

So when he started talking, he quietly spoke eight statements that painted a different picture than the one they had envisioned, but a perfect roadmap for becoming like the Son of God. Those statements ring as true today as they did then.

Until we take the time to learn humility, mourn in brokenness, practice surrender, embrace dependence, be merciful, live authentically, pursue peace, and focus on eternity, we cannot take on the social, ethical, and political issues in our day.

The most important work is never what God is doing *out there*, but what He is doing *in me*. When I take these eight steps, my relationship with God and people flourish. This means most of the issues Jesus is going to address next take care of themselves.

Our problem is not with the law but with our hearts. We are trying to fix problems in our culture but neglecting the condition of our hearts. We must allow God to change our hearts first.

This is where Jesus began and what he stayed focused on throughout his ministry.

It must be where we begin if we hope to be salt and light in a very dark world.

PART II

Recommit to Impacting Culture

(Engaging Culture with Faith)

Introduction

Love Over Laws

First words, like first impressions, are powerful. Jesus is 30 years old and about to begin his public ministry.

He announces his intention one afternoon in the temple (Luke 4).

He is publicly inaugurated by John "The Baptizer" in the Jordan river (Matthew 3).

Now Jesus stands to give his inaugural address of sorts with The Sermon on the Mount (Matthew 5-7). If Jesus is going to redeem a fallen and broken world, where should he start?

This sermon would establish a framework for his life and ministry. So what he said would be critical.

As the first words of his ministry leave his mouth and echo down the Galilean hillside, Jesus makes a couple of things clear. First, the difficult job of redeeming our world begins in our hearts.

Second, the life we are looking for is dependent on developing a thriving relationship with God and each other. No matter what else we accomplish, if our relationships with God and each other fail, we will never be happy. The blessing comes from being part of his spiritual family.

Third, there are political, social, and cultural issues everywhere, but they are the *symptoms*, not the problem. These issues are the fruit of our failure to love God and each other. If our relationships with God and other people are healthy, most of these issues take care of themselves.

If our relationships are failing, there is not a natural, spiritual, or political law strong enough to address all these problems in our culture. In fact, these laws usually lead to loopholes we use to excuse our selfishness and immorality, which damages our relationship with God and each other. Religious people may have been looking for a religious or political solution, but Jesus understood the source of the problem—our hearts.

Therefore, Jesus begins the Sermon on the Mount with the Beatitudes and describes how to be blessed in a way that would have immediately captured people's attention. As the previous section of this book indicates, the Beatitudes describe how to establish a healthy relationship with God and how to love each other.

Jesus began by immediately trying to cut through all the religious confusion, because sometimes we cannot see the forest for the trees. We can miss our connection with God and each other when we are blinded by religion.

Jesus wants to simplify and solidify our faith.

That's what makes the story in Matthew 22, when an expert in religious law asked Jesus about the most important commandment, so powerful. Love God, and love your neighbor as yourself.

To Jesus, it's as simple and complex as that.

In America, we have millions of pages of laws but a problem with lawlessness. The answer to this problem is not another law. We do not have a legislative problem, we have a heart problem. As I work on this draft, racial division has flared up again, and people all over the country are proposing new laws to defeat racism.

For years we have seen a growing political divide as both sides of Congress have proposed new legislation to prevent the other side from "destroying" our country. We are in the midst of a global pandemic, and in order to "save us all" from the pandemic we have people at every level of government proposing social rules for stopping the spread of COVID-19, while others propose laws to defend individual freedoms. The pandemic has thrown America back into a recession, and we are creating legislation to "save the economy".

Sound familiar?

If Jesus was here, this is what he would say: *Write all the laws you want, but until people learn to receive my love and share it with each other, the laws will not fix your problems.* As long as our relationship with God and with each other is not healthy, if we do not learn to love one another, our solutions will fail.

No matter what we accomplish, no matter our prosperity, we will not be happy.

We will not be blessed.

In the West, often Jesus is a means to an end. We want Jesus to do something for us or get something for us so we can be happy. We attempt to use Jesus, but we have not learned to love him. Therefore, we attempt to use each other, because we have not learned to love.

This is why Jesus begins with the Beatitudes.

By addressing our relationship with God and each other *before* addressing the pressing social, moral, and ethical issues of his day, Jesus's first words quickly cut to the root of the problem.

Two millennia later, this is where we have to start.

The Beatitudes describe a spiritual journey and a map for how to develop a thriving relationship with Jesus and how to love each other. The first four Beatitudes describe our spiritual posture before God—humility, brokenness, surrender, and dependence. The second four Beatitudes describe how we can love each other—mercy, authenticity, peace, and perspective in the face of persecution.

When our relationships with God and each other are healthy, most of the moral, ethical, social, and political issues take care of themselves. Jesus knew that you cannot change the world with a law!

- You cannot be salt and light with a law.
- You cannot live a holy life with a law.
- You cannot overcome hate with a law.
- You cannot overcome lust with a law.
- You cannot overcome divorce with a law.
- You cannot overcome lying with a law.
- You cannot overcome revenge with a law.
- You cannot defeat your enemies with a law.
- You cannot live generously with a law.
- You cannot pray according to a law.
- You cannot overcome materialism with a law.
- You cannot overcome judgment with a law.

This is why Jesus came.

Jesus entered into our brokenness to redeem our lives and transform our world.

And in the next very practical section of the Sermon on the Mount, Jesus shows us how it's love, not laws that help you become like Jesus.

CHAPTER NINE

Be Bright and Flavorful

Act as Salt and Light

When Jesus looked at his world, he saw it through spiritual eyes.

He saw the pain and darkness that crippled creation.

Through these eyes, Jesus understood that a *rule* would not bring healing and light to a broken and dark world. However, if we could learn to love God and each other, *that* would change everything.

The message may be centuries old, but its power and need are still just as strong today.

Into this pain and darkness, Jesus invites us to be the salt and light of the world. When we love God and love each other, we bring healing and light. When we fail to love God and each other, we contribute to the pain and darkness.

Jesus declared, "The Lord is upon me, for He has anointed me to bring Good News to the poor. He has sent me to proclaim that captives will be released, that the blind will see, that the oppressed will be set free, and that the time of the Lord's favor has come." This sounds like a revolution!

When Jesus looked around, he could see poverty and the pain poverty inflicts. He could see the bondage that shackled the people. He could see the physical, spiritual, and social blindness in Israel. He knew firsthand the oppression the Jews were living under.

Into this pain Jesus made a declaration: *I have come to do something about all this!*

We have heard that before, right? A politician looks at a nation's problems and makes unrealistic, arrogant promises that he or she usually knows they are incapable of fulfilling just to be elected.

Jesus is no politician.

He makes some bold promises, but his strategy is unique.

Jesus understands what good leaders know: If you fix the problem without addressing the cause, in short order you will simply recreate the problem. The pain and darkness we experience is a reflection of the condition of our hearts. What we see is not the problem but the symptom.

The problem is the fruit of your behavior, and your behavior is a reflection of your heart. Therefore, work must begin in our hearts. If we begin with the cause—the heart—then we can change behavior and produce better outcomes. We can eliminate the pain and darkness. This is what Jesus means when he says we are the salt and light of the world. When we love God and love each other, we bring healing into the pain and light into the darkness.

Jesus says, "What good is salt if it has lost its flavor? Can you make it salty again?"

He asked this for good reason—the Jews had lost their flavor. It was difficult to distinguish them from the culture around them. They had lost their spiritual vitality. They were religious, but that distinction was more cultural than spiritual.

Sound familiar?

Salt without saltiness is useless.

Religion that doesn't result in a relationship is too.

Right from the start, Jesus spoke in stories and parables he knew his audience would understand. He wanted his message to be understood by all who came in contact with it. They would have understood salt because in the first century, salt had at least four purposes.

First, salt was **a preserving agent.** Before modern refrigeration, salt was applied to meat to prevent spoiling. In the same way, when we love God and love each other, our love for one another holds back the destructive moral corruption in society. If we were to make a list of all the moral, ethical, and social problems we are facing as a nation, it would be relatively easy to cast them as a failure to love.

Second, salt **promotes healing.** As a kid, if I busted my lip my mom would tell me to rinse my mouth out with a little saltwater. It stung like crazy, but that salt would promote healing. When we love God and love each other, it brings healing to our world. Right now, we have people who are hurting from a global pandemic and racial injustice, but our love is a healing agent. This is why over the last few months we have been feeding the hungry and listening to the hurting. Driven by love, we want to be a healing agent in our city.

Third, salt **provides flavor.** Adding salt to just about anything makes it taste better! What if people said that about Christians? Add a Christian to any situation, any team, any neighborhood, any company, or any relationship, and they make it better! That's what Jesus had in mind.

Finally, salt **makes a person thirsty.** We have all heard the saying, "You can lead a horse to water, but you cannot make him drink." That saying is not entirely true. Give that horse a little salt, and he will drink.

What if all our relationships made people thirsty? What if being around Christians produced a strong desire to *be with Jesus, to become like Jesus, and to do what Jesus did?*

This is what Jesus wants for us. Remember the context. Jesus isn't giving his sermon to usher in a new program, but rather to demonstrate *the natural result* of learning to love God and love each other.

Jesus's teaching always seemed simple but had many layers to discover.

That's why there are two less obvious characteristics of salt that are implied in this passage.

First, salt must be pure. I live in Greensboro, North Carolina, and each winter we get a little snow and freezing rain. When we are expecting freezing precipitation, trucks drive around spreading "salt" on the roads. However, if you have ever been behind a salt truck, you may have seen that the salt being spread is not white. That is because the salt used on roads has not been taken through the purification process and contains mineral impurities. Imagine putting that on your steak!

It would add flavor and crunch; however, you would be eating dirt. No one puts impure salt on their food. If the salt is impure, Jesus says it is good for nothing but to be thrown out and walked on.

When our lives are impure, we fail to love God and each other, and our impact is minimal.

Christians in America typically look at our culture—much as I suspect the Jews looked at their culture—and wonder why it is so confused, immoral, and violent. Maybe it is because the American church has grown impure and dim. We're salt without the saltiness.

If this is true, rather than providing protection, healing, and flavor, the best we can hope for is to be thrown on the ground to keep people from crashing.

A religious organization provides rules to live by so people do not wander outside the guardrails. Jesus has so much more in mind for us.

Not only does salt need to be pure; it also needs to be applied.

A couple of years ago we were hit by a large and unexpected snowstorm. Although we had plenty of salt for the roads, it was too late, and the snow was falling too fast to get it out. The salt was good, but unapplied it was useless, and the roads became a slick, icy mess.

If the salt represents my life, it is critical for me to be closely connected to those who need protection, healing, flavor, and thirst *before* the storm comes. As Christians, we cannot hide in our churches while the world falls apart. If your life is pure and connected, then you are the salt of the earth! Your life has the capacity to provide protection, healing, and flavor.

It increases everyone's appetite for Jesus!

In 1992, I was a sophomore in college and had a financial crisis. At the time, I was living on my own and (barely) financially independent. My car broke down, which may not be that big of a deal for most people, but I delivered pizza for a living. I needed to keep working but did not have the money to fix my car.

I had to make a tough choice. I dropped out of college, got my tuition money back, and used the money to fix my car. I hoped to jump back into school as soon as possible, but I wasn't sure when that would be.

A couple of weeks later, I had two incredible conversations. First, a widow in our church who worked with the youth group and lived in a large house reached out to me. She said she had a big house, plenty of room, and could use a little help. She offered to let me live with her if I would help around the house. It was an amazing blessing!

Then another man in the church reached out. He told me he heard I had dropped out of college, but he believed I had a call on my life. He told me if I would get back in school, he would pay for my last two years!

In the midst of my darkness, the light of the church was shining bright! Their bright faith in me brought financial protection, relational healing, allowed me to taste generosity, and produced a greater spiritual hunger in my life!

The light they shined on my life helped me grow into the man I am today.

Jesus says, you are the light of the world, and a light always chases away the darkness.

Jeremiah Johnson, in his book *Unimaginable*, says,

There was much to fear in the ancient world. By today's standards, it was hell on earth. Poverty, sickness, premature death, domestic violence, economic injustice, slavery, and political corruption were a given. Absent were any ideas of justice, equality, mercy, democracy, education, and protection of the weak and marginalized. All this started to change when people began living with a sense of the divine, and a sense of God's presence.

Throughout history, Christianity has been light in a very dark world. In fact, Johnson demonstrates that it is "unimaginable" just how dark the world would be without the light of Christianity.

The apostle John walked with Jesus, so it's no surprise that he said Jesus is, "the light shining in the darkness, and the darkness can never extinguish it." Christianity has dramatically reduced pain and suffering throughout history and around the world.

Jesus says we are that light.

We are a city on a hill whose light gives hope, safety, and direction to everyone around us.

When I look back on my own life, it was in my darkest moments when the light of Christ—shining through the life of one of his followers—helped me find my way through the darkness.

When we love Jesus and each other, our light shines in a dark world, and we can't help but make the world a better place. Jesus did this everywhere he went. After finishing this message, the first person he encountered was living in the darkness of leprosy, a terminal and highly- contagious skin disease.

When a person contracted leprosy, they lost everything. They were isolated permanently from their family, kids, and community. They could no longer work, go to church, or even be around other people. When they were near other people, they would have to announce their presence and physical condition by shouting, "unclean, unclean".

It was a devastatingly lonely life.

Jesus saw him with spiritual eyes. He saw the hurt and loneliness and fear.

But what he did next demonstrated that Jesus was radically, truly different.

He reached out and *touched the man* that society had deemed unclean and healed Him.

Next, Jesus encounters a Roman officer whose servant was bedridden, paralyzed, and in terrible pain. The officer asks Jesus to help, and Jesus responds. For the rest of his ministry, Jesus goes on to heal many people, to calm the storm, and to deliver the demoniac.

Over and over again, Jesus enters into the darkness, and his light dispels the darkness.

He was salt—he made things flavorful.

He was light—he made things brighter.

Like Jesus, we are to be the light of the world.

God invites us to step into the darkness and display our light for all to see. When we live in humility, brokenness, surrender, and dependence, we bring into our world mercy, authenticity, and peace.

The light of the gospel shining through our lives dispels the darkness and makes the world better and brighter. And that's what this world is longing for.

CHAPTER TEN

Be Righteous

Keep the Law

E arly one Sunday morning I got up and headed to church. I usually try to be at the church by six o'clock, and in the winter it is still dark.

At the time, the church was really growing. We were in a small building that seated about 100 people, and we were doing three services. We always ran out of parking, so our staff usually parked in the grass. However, that morning it was raining, and as I pulled into the grass, it felt too soft. I was afraid I was going to get stuck, so I circled around to find a parking space on the pavement.

Meanwhile, a sheriff's deputy was driving by and saw me making a slow circle in the churchyard. He was concerned some teenager was potentially vandalizing the church property, so as I was headed to my parking space, he pulled in behind me with his blue lights flashing.

I was so naive that I did not even consider that he was "policing me". I thought he needed help, so rather than stopping my car, I circled around to pull beside him and see if I could help. After all, it was raining, I was in my church clothes, and even though I wanted to be helpful, I did not want to stand in the rain. I thought if I swung around we could both roll our window down and talk to each other without having to get wet. It made sense to me.

Well, he did not appreciate that.

He thought I was being aggressive, so he pulled around behind me again.

I was a small-town pastor, and I had never been in trouble with the law. Since I was on our church property, it still had not dawned on me that he thought I could be a drunk person, vandalizing the parking lot and now responding to him in a threatening manner.

As I watched him speed up to head me off, I started thinking to myself, *what is this idiot doing?* (Of course, looking back, I realize I was the idiot in this story.) Undeterred, I proceeded once again to attempt to circle around to talk to the officer without either one of us having to stand in the rain.

I assumed I was being a thoughtful, considerate, and helpful citizen.

For some reason, the officer did not see it that way.

Apparently, he'd had enough.

He whipped his car back around behind me again, jumped out, drew his firearm, and started shouting orders at me. This is the only time I have ever had a gun pointed at me, and it was terrifying. The next few moments were tense, but once I explained to the officer I was the pastor, and he chewed me out for not following his instructions, he let me go, and I lived to preach another day.

The problem that day was simple—he did not know who I was or why I was there, and this led to confusion and misunderstanding. The same problem was true when Jesus started his ministry.

No one really knew who he was or why he was there.

With the Sermon on the Mount, that was all about to change.

Jesus climbed the hillside and planted his flag in the ground. He wanted no confusion.

"Don't misunderstand why I have come!" Jesus knew he would be different from anything they had ever seen, and consequently, he was often misunderstood. Jesus was considered a liberal and a rebel for not following the traditions of the Pharisees.

Here's an example. The fourth commandment is "Honor the Sabbath." The Sabbath was Saturday and to be a day of rest. In order to make sure no one broke this command, the Pharisees came up with 39 categories of activities that they considered work and therefore a violation of the Sabbath.

They meant well. They were trying to obey the command, but this legalistic, independent strategy for obedience shifted everyone's focus away from the *relationship* God desired to nurture on the Sabbath to the *rule*. When Jesus healed a man on the Sabbath, these lawmakers were so obsessed with their rule that they lost sight of the heart of God and His love for people.

Jesus understood the value of keeping God's law.

He also understood that God's law is God's attempt to protect and bless His children.

In these verses in Matthew, Jesus makes four powerful points about the law.

First, Jesus came to *accomplish* **the law**. Jesus lived a perfect, sinless, holy life. He never violated any of God's commands. Hebrews 4:15 says, "Jesus was tempted in every way, just like we are, yet without sin." This is why Jesus was able to take our place on the cross and die for our sin. Paul says, "For God made Christ, *who never sinned*, to be the offering for our sin, so that we could be made right with God through Christ" (2 Corinthians 5:21). Jesus was perfect, holy, and sinless which is why he was able to die in our place. He did this to accomplish the law.

Second, Jesus came to **fulfill the prophets.** In the Old Testament, there are over 300 prophecies and predictions about the Messiah. Jesus fulfilled *every one* of those prophecies which were outside of his control. For example, the prophets said the Messiah would be born of a virgin, born in Bethlehem, betrayed for thirty pieces of silver, and resurrected from the dead. These are prophecies Jesus could only fulfill if he was the one the prophets spoke of (Isaiah 53).

Third, Jesus came to **raise our standard of morality,** not lower it. One of the problems with laws is loopholes. When faced with a law, our tendency is to find a way to break it, invalidate it, or to find an exception to the rule. We live in a culture that rejects moral absolutes and celebrates immorality. Jesus did not come to destroy or invalidate the law, nor to find a loophole. He didn't come to lower God's expectations but to raise them. Jesus rejects even the slightest moral compromise.

Why?

Because Jesus understands that sin breaks relationships. Jesus wants to protect our relationships with him and with each other. Jesus says not even the smallest part of the law will be set aside or outdated. *All* will be fulfilled, and only Jesus could fulfill it. Jesus did not come to throw out the law but to set us free from sin as we learn to be with Jesus, become like Jesus, and do what Jesus did.

That often brings up a point of confusion though.

If Jesus did not abolish the law, why are there so many laws in the Old Testament that we no longer follow? That is a great question. One way to understand which laws carry over into the

New Testament is to categorize the Old Testament law into three types: sacrificial law, ceremonial law, and moral law.

The sacrificial laws were those that regulated the sacrificial system. The reason we no longer observe the sacrificial laws is that Jesus fulfilled the sacrificial law through his death and resurrection. Jesus offered his blood, once and for all, to pay for our sin (Hebrews 10:10).

The ceremonial laws were the laws that set the Jews apart as God's chosen people. These laws distinguished them from all the other people on earth and include rules about circumcision and diet. The reason we no longer observe the ceremonial laws is that Jesus tore down the distinction between Jews and Gentiles (Ephesians 2:11-13, Galatians 3:28) and brought us all into one family. In the New Testament, the new distinguishing mark of Christians is the Holy Spirit and the fruit of the Spirit (Ephesians 1:16, 1 Corinthians 6:19, Romans 8, Matthew 7:16-20, Galatians 5:22).

The third category is moral law. Moral laws govern our relationship with God and each other. Jesus makes it clear throughout the Sermon on the Mount that the moral law is still very much in effect. This makes sense since he came to strengthen our relationships. Not only does he confirm the moral law, but he also raises the expectations by saying it is not enough to simply conform to a law in public.

Jesus wants your heart.

My behavior is a reflection of my heart. My behavior is an expression or a violation of love. When I learn to be with Jesus, I become like him, which empowers me to do what Jesus did. This is what Jesus came to accomplish. In our culture today, we have a tendency to treat the moral law like a moral buffet.

I can embrace and obey what I agree with, embrace and obey what feels good, but in doing so, I am playing God. I am not surrendered or living in dependence. Instead, *I* am in charge; *I* decide right from wrong, and *I* have declared my independence. This is exactly what Adam and Eve did in the garden, and, well, that didn't turn out any better for them than it will for you. This is the fruit of our sinful nature, and this is the cause of the pain and suffering in our world.

Finally, the law **exposes our need for a savior** (Romans 3:19-20). How do you know if a line is crooked? The easy answer is by holding it up to something that is straight. The law is that straight line. It's why the Bible seems like a list of dos and don'ts to so many people. But it plays a vital role—it exposes our sinfulness and, most importantly, our need for Jesus.

Paul says the law arouses my sinful nature and produces death in me, but the Spirit leads me into life (Romans 7-8)! That is what Jesus came to accomplish. My inability to keep the law does not mean the law is bad; it means I need God's help (Romans 7:19)! The problem comes when we struggle to keep the law, and we start to reject the law. Since it's hard to keep the law on our own, we claim it is irrelevant or out of date. When we rebel, we encourage others to join us in our immorality. We start saying things like *God understands, God wants me to be happy*, or *God made me this way*, rather than recognizing that Jesus came to save us from our sin and set us free from its control over us. Jesus is giving us a strong warning—do not make excuses for immorality, and do not encourage others to join you in your immorality.

Jesus came to free us from the law. In verse twenty, Jesus says, *unless your righteousness is better than the teachers of religious law and the Pharisees, you will never enter the kingdom of heaven.*

Think about how radical this statement is!

This would be like saying unless your righteousness surpasses the righteousness of Billy Graham or Mother Teresa, you are not going to Heaven. If that is true, then we should either give up or be in a complete panic, because none of us believe we are more righteous than Billy Graham or Mother Teresa.

That is exactly how everyone must have felt when they heard Jesus say this.

Jesus came to speak the uncomfortable truth: you cannot go to heaven unless you are perfect. This begs the question then, how can any of us possibly go to heaven? Only through the death and resurrection of Jesus! It is not what we have done, but what Christ has done for us! I am reminded of that old hymn, *Nothing but the Blood of Jesus*. It goes like this:

What can wash away my sin? Nothing but the blood of Jesus; What can make me whole again? Nothing but the blood of Jesus. Oh! precious is the flow That makes me white as snow; No other fount I know, Nothing but the blood of Jesus.

This is the good news! Jesus came to do for us what we could never do for ourselves. Jesus came to fulfill the law for us so that we can have a relationship with the Father and live with Him in Heaven forever.

Just read through this quick list of encouraging verses:

- "Therefore, since we have been justified through faith, we have peace with God through our Lord Jesus Christ" (Romans 5:1).

- "We all, like sheep, have gone astray, each of us has turned to our own way, and the LORD has laid on him (Jesus) the iniquity of us all" (Isaiah 53:6).

- "Christ suffered for our sins once for all time. He never sinned, but he died for sinners to bring you safely home to God" (1 Peter 3:18).

- "For it is by grace you have been saved, through faith—and this is not from yourselves, it is the gift of God—not by works, so that no one can boast" (Ephesians 2:8-9).

Jesus came to set us free from the law!

Religion says, clean up your life so you can get close to God. Jesus said get close to me, and I will clean up your life. When we learn to be with Jesus, we become like him, and then it is natural to do what he did. We do not try to clean our lives up so Jesus will accept us. No matter how hard you scrub, you'll never wash away the stain of your sin.

And you don't have to anyway.

Jesus paid for our sin so we can be close to Him. When we get close to him, he cleans our life up, and when he cleans up our life we begin to do what he did. Jesus begins this work in our hearts. Ezekiel 36:25-27 puts it this way:

Then I will sprinkle clean water on you and you will be clean. Your filth will be washed away and you will no longer worship idols. And I will give you a new heart and I will put a new spirit in you. I will take out your stony, stubborn heart and give you a tender, responsive heart. And I will put my Spirit in you so that you will follow my decrees and be careful to obey my regulations.

If you are feeling trapped by the law and constrained by the impossibility of doing what it says, take heart, Jesus will wash you clean! Jesus will give you a new heart, He will change your desires. Jesus will give you his Spirit to lead and guide you into a blessed life!

This is the power of the gospel—when we understand what God has done for us through His son Jesus and turn to Him in faith. He forgives us, gives us a new heart, and places His Spirit in us so we can live the Christian life.

This life is not based on fear and rules, but on love and delight.

This life is not based on willpower, but on the Spirit's power in me.

Jesus said, "All who love me will do what I say. My Father will love them, and we will come and make our home with each of them. Anyone who doesn't love me will not obey me" (John 14:23-24).

Furthermore, when we love God, His love for other people grows in our hearts. We cannot claim to love God and yet hate people (1 John 4:7-19). This is why, before addressing the moral, ethical, and social issues of his day, Jesus begins with our love for God and each other. I don't know about you, but I'd love to see a world where the people who claim to love God prove it by showing how much they love people.

If we love God and each other, then *everything else falls into place* (Matthew 22:34-40).

Christians are not perfect.

However, they have been forgiven. Christians have been given a new heart, which means they *want to do the right thing*. They are growing in love. They have the Holy Spirit, a gracious, faithful, gentle friend that continues to lead them into healing, freedom, and power (1 John 3:4-10).

Jesus did not come to throw out the rules.

Jesus came to fulfill the law so we can have eternal life.

Jesus came to free us from the law so we can have abundant life now.

CHAPTER ELEVEN

Be Calm

Guard Against Anger

It doesn't take a genius to sense it. It's right there, seemingly below the surface of everything, just waiting to flare up.

It seems America is angry about everything. But why?

We live in one of the richest countries in the world. We have freedoms that other people routinely give their lives to try and attain. We are mostly well-fed, well-housed, well-clothed, and well-stocked. We seemingly have all we need.

And yet anger threatens to destroy us. Why?

One reason we are angry is that we were created for paradise, and this is clearly not it. Even though most of us are well-fed, well-housed, and well-clothed, many others are hungry and homeless. Sometimes good loses and evil wins. We long for paradise but have to settle for the pain of a broken world.

We were made for more.

We were created to live a blessed life.

We were created to be connected to God and each other, and when we are disconnected, we eventually become very angry (Romans

1:18-32). This is one of the dangers of religion. Often religious people are legalistic, mean-spirited, judgmental, hypocritical, and angry.

Jesus wasn't religious, so his anger, when it appeared, was well-warranted.

Jesus invites us into a life characterized by grace, mercy, peace, and love.

Remember, he did not come to lower the moral standards but to raise them. Jesus described, in the Beatitudes, what it looks like to have a healthy relationship with God and how to love each other.

Now, Jesus turns his attention to the big social issues of his day, each time beginning with the phrase, *you've heard it said... but now I say to you...* Jesus has come to change the world, and that means going beyond the minimum. In each of these statements, Jesus makes it clear that following the rule is not enough.

A rule will not stop hate, lust, selfishness, lying, nor any of the other sins that plague us.

Only a changed heart can do that, and Jesus wants to change our hearts.

The focus of these next six statements (which I'll talk about in the next six chapters) illustrates the difference between religion— following the rules, doing what you can—and following Christ. Following Christ begins with being with him. Being with Jesus means connecting with him and living in his presence each day. When we learn to be with him, we supernaturally become like him. Becoming like him means letting the life of Jesus transform us from the inside out. When we become like Jesus, we are empowered to face the ethical issues we face every day. We are empowered to do what Jesus did!

It is not enough to just follow the rules most of the time and in public.

Jesus wants to transform our hearts and produce integrity in our lives.

He wants our public and private life to match.

He wants us to live from our heart, empowered by the Spirit.

The first issue Jesus addresses is anger, and the first thing Jesus says is when we are angry we must admit it. What Jesus understands is this—*unresolved* anger is like murder because it kills relationships. Denying or ignoring our anger is like sitting on a lit stick of dynamite. It may not blow up for a while, but when it does, the outcome is catastrophic.

The truth is, anger is not all bad—*if* it's addressed and dealt with.

Anger is our emotional response to feeling out of control. Anger can be a very positive force in our relationships. In fact, if you look back on your closest relationships, often the breakthrough moment was when someone got angry, and it forced you to deal with an issue that was harming the relationship but previously went unaddressed.

Anger can be the impetus that leads to healthier relationships, healthier organizations, and healthier families. Anger is a flag, a signal that indicates we need to do something about this! Christians do not like to admit that they are angry. We do not like to admit we are angry because in many Christian circles, that is "unspiritual."

But this is unbiblical and, frankly, ridiculous.

Jesus got angry. In John 2, Jesus gets so angry that he makes a weapon, a whip, and drives the money changers out of the temple. Jesus is angry (and rightfully so!) because these people have become a *barrier* between God and these people when they were supposed to be a *bridge*. Jesus got angry, and you are going to get angry. In fact, injustice anywhere should make you angry. However, in our anger, we do not have to sin (Ephesians 4:26).

Some people think being sappy and nice is a sign of Christian maturity.

The truth is, this type of person is either faking it or they are people pleasers. Either way, they are not being honest and living out of their heart. What looks like maturity is actually a sign of their immaturity.

In fact, this is one of the reasons many men do not like church. They think the goal of church is to make them nice, quiet, polite, and passive, when the reality is God wants self-assured men of courage who can change the world. Sometimes, we need to get angry to get things done.

If anger is my emotional response to feeling like I am losing control, then I should ask myself two questions:

- *Do I have a legitimate right to control this situation or person?*
- *Is this situation important enough to get angry about?*

If someone cuts you off driving home today, you can ask yourself these questions. Should I expect to control how other people drive, and is this important enough to get angry over? The answer to both questions is *no.* Therefore, there is no legitimate reason to be angry.

What if a guest at your home backs out of the driveway, drives in your yard by accident, and messes up the grass? This happened to me recently, and I take a lot of pride in my yard. Should I expect to control if people ride in my grass? Yes! Is a little smashed down grass important enough to be angry with a friend? No! My relationship is more important than my yard.

What if your kids are being noisy when you are trying to go to sleep? Do I have the right to control the noise level in my house at night? Yes! Is the noise my family is making worth damaging our relationships? No! I just put in earplugs and go to sleep.

What if one of your kids wrecks the car? Do you have the right, when you own the car and pay the insurance, to control the driving habits of your kids? Yes! However, is an accident worth getting angry over? No, that is why I have insurance.

If we will simply ask these two questions when we start to feel anger bubbling up, then it becomes obvious that most of what we are angry about is unjustified.

The next thing Jesus teaches us about anger is this—when I get angry, I need to do something about it. I need to go to the person I am angry with in order to work out our disagreement. I need to be merciful, authentic, and a peacemaker. Jesus says, if you are in church and remember someone has something against you, stop whatever you are doing, and as an act of worship go be reconciled to your brother. We cannot love God and yet attack people in our anger.

Most of us have a problem with this, because, quite frankly, sometimes it feels good to be mad. We sit in our anger feeling justified and use it to fuel our thoughts. It may feel good in the moment, but it *kills relationships* with others and, perhaps more devastatingly, with God.

If we are not careful, we will sit in church each week while our relationships are a mess. When you are angry, you need to do something with your anger. If you stuff your feelings inside and try to keep a lid on that box, eventually you will lash out and potentially destroy the relationship.

When we are angry, we must talk about it and work it out, or we block our ability to worship.

Worship is your way of loving God. When we sing, when we serve, and when we give, we are expressing our love and gratitude to God. Jesus's message is simple: if you want to worship me, love each other.

I have three kids, and one of the best ways they can express their love for me is to *love each other*. We cannot love God and still remain angry or even hate each other. That does not mean we will not get angry with each other. We will. Sometimes love is tough love. But what it does mean is this—when we commit to dealing with our anger, we *value the relationship* more than what we are angry about. We come together to work it out. We do not avoid each other or attack one another from a distance or on social media.

I have been a pastor for 21 years, 19 of those years at Definition Church. Every time a church conflict has blown up and caused people to leave the church, there has always been one common denominator—*the people who were angry were unwilling to talk about it.* They were unwilling to sit down and talk to the church leadership, church staff, trustees, or overseers about their concerns. Unfortunately, because we did not talk, the conflict was left unresolved and people were hurt and divided.

What do you think happens to those emotions they are feeling? They take them with them to their next church where they fester and grow unchecked. This must break Jesus's heart—he wants unity among believers so we can share him with the world.

If someone is upset with me, and I know about it, I need to reach out to them. If someone has offended me, I need to reach out to them (Matthew 18:21-35). Sometimes we have to agree to disagree, but for the sake of the kingdom, we have to lay aside our petty differences in order to reach people for Christ. Jesus prayed,

"I pray that they may be one...so the world will know you sent me" (John 17:21). Sometimes, we do all we can, but the other person refuses to do the right thing, and we have to move on. Romans 12:18 says, "As much as it is up to you, live at peace with all men."

When we are angry, we need to settle it quickly (Matthew 5:25). The longer we wait to deal with our anger, typically, the worse things get. When we get angry with someone we will probably never see again, we can blow it off and move on. When we get angry with the people in our lives, we see all the time an attempt to blow it off or sweep it under the rug doesn't usually work. It often builds up until it leads to an explosion.

This is what happened in my marriage. Tina and I dated for years and had the same issues the entire time we were dating. However, when we got married and moved away, the pressure brought our issues to the surface.

For the first five months of our marriage, Tina tried to stuff her anger in a box until finally, she exploded. The explosion wasn't fun, and there was collateral damage, but at least after the smoke cleared and she admitted she was angry, we knew we had a problem, and we could do something about it.

When you have conflict, the sooner you deal with it the better.

Take the rip-the-Band-Aid-off approach. It stings at first, but then you address the wound.

Now, when Tina and I talk about something, she may need some time to think about it before she decides how she feels, and that is fine. But we always try to get the conversation started as soon as possible. Paul says:

Therefore, having put away falsehood, let each one of you speak the truth with his neighbor, for we are members of one another. Be angry and do not sin; do not let the sun go down on your anger, and give no opportunity to the devil... Let no corrupting talk come out of your mouths, but only such as is good for building up, as fits the occasion, that it may give grace to those who hear. And do not grieve the Holy Spirit of God, by whom you were sealed for the day of redemption. Let all bitterness and wrath and anger and clamor and slander be put away from you, along with all malice. Be kind to one another, tenderhearted, forgiving one another, as God in Christ forgave you (Ephesians 4:25-27, 29-32).

There's one more thing to consider about anger. When we are angry, we need God's help. Jesus does not want us to be satisfied with the fact that we have not killed anyone lately. That's a pretty low bar to attain, and Jesus has a higher plan—he wants us to love each other.

When we ask God to help us put away our anger, we can get about the business of love.

CHAPTER TWELVE

Be Pure

Protect Against Lust

Y ou would think (hope?) that a newly-licensed minister who was preparing to go to seminary, engaged to be married, with a dream of being a pastor, would not have a pornography problem.

You would be wrong.

Sexual immorality almost destroyed me.

Publicly, I was a Christian on track to do big things for God.

Privately, I had a *purity* problem. I'd been exposed to pornography at a very early age, and it only got worse as I got into my teens and early adulthood. By the time I got to college, with a roommate with a huge stash of porn, it didn't take much for me to get hooked. I'd spend my days depressed, looking at porn, questioning my ministry call and even my salvation. I was overwhelmed with guilt, shame, and hopelessness.

It's like I was stuck in quicksand.

Finally, in desperation, I spoke to my roommate, and he agreed to throw out all the porn. This was before computers or cell phones, so with the magazines gone, I was free! Or so I thought.

I went on to graduate from UNCW, started seminary, and married Tina. Life was great again. However, five months into our marriage, Tina and I were in trouble, so we dropped out of seminary to focus all our attention on strengthening our young and fragile marriage.

We moved back to Wilmington, where I went to work for Sears selling TVs and the new home computers which had just come on the market. With my employee discount, I bought my first home computer and guess what happened?

Before long, I was looking at porn again.

The computer made it so easy. It was free, and I could look at it in the privacy of my home. This was back in the days of dial-up internet when it took 15 to 30 seconds for a picture to load on the screen and the same time to clear the screen. One night, Tina caught me looking at porn and was understandably crushed.

It was one of the most heartbreaking moments of my life.

I was on the verge of losing the two things that mattered to me—my wife and my ministry.

Looking back, I can see with clarity the frustrating truth—my sexual sin did not produce happiness in my life. Quite the opposite—my sexual immorality produced regret, shame, relational dysfunction, depression, addiction, unrealistic sexual expectations, and a score of other problems. That was twenty-four years ago.

Today, we live in a culture where sexual temptation is stronger than ever, and yet thanks to the grace of God, I am free. My marriage is great. My sex life with Tina is great. Sexual purity is a blessing but something I have to keep fighting for.

The most recent studies show that one out of every two people—*50 percent*— attending church are looking at or could be addicted to internet pornography. It gets worse. Nine out of ten boys and six out of ten girls are exposed to porn before the age of 18. Sixty-eight percent of young adult men watch porn at least once a week.

It's not a stretch to say that you may be part of this struggle.

Let me be clear: speaking from experience, I can say that you are on the verge of losing *everything* that is important to you. Porn, lust, and sexual addiction can cost you your spouse, your kids, your career, your financial security, and even your health and safety.

If you struggle with purity, then deep down you probably already know that you're walking a fine and dangerous line. You may feel trapped, hopeless, desperate, and afraid. However, there is hope. Jesus can change everything!

In my moment of desperation, God met me and changed my life.

That was the moment when I learned the difference between religion and a life-changing relationship with Jesus. As a seminary student preparing to be a pastor, I was proud of my ability to keep the big rules; I was not committing physical adultery, but my heart was full of lust.

Outside, I looked good. Inside, my heart was a mess.

Publicly, it looked like I had it all together. Privately, I was barely holding on.

You may be barely holding on. If so, the question is: Are you going to settle for religion when Jesus came to set you free and lead you into abundant life?

Religion is legalistic, mean-spirited, judgmental, hypocritical, and impersonal. It does not produce purity, it produces hypocrisy. Religion causes us to hide. This is why Jesus says the pure in heart—the spiritually and morally authentic—are blessed. When we stop hiding and bring our lust and other issues to Jesus, he will lead us into freedom and a blessed life.

Jesus is not legalistic, mean-spirited, judgmental, hypocritical, and impersonal.

Jesus is gracious.

Jesus is full of love and compassion, and if you will follow him, he will empower you to live a pure and happy life! When your relationship with Jesus and others is flourishing, your determination to defeat lust overwhelms your desire for immorality. Rather than protecting your sin, you protect your purity so you can honor your relationships.

Jesus came to set us free! However, we live in a world that says the key to happiness is *moral* freedom. The world says, "If it feels good, do it!" The world says we must break free from the moral *shackles* of religion. In fact, some even argue that much of the mental illness in our culture, like depression, anxiety, and suicide, are caused not by the sinfulness of man, but by the guilt and shame religion has produced in our hearts.

I have been a pastor for twenty-one years, and I have never met anyone who pursued immorality and found happiness. It always leaves you empty, desperate, and broken. Ironically, religion and hedonism both leave you empty. God wants a relationship to maximize your delight, joy, and happiness.

Jesus came to raise the standards and our expectations for life.

Jesus came to empower us to live in freedom and blessing.

But first, we must have purity of heart.

Purity is a Reflection of the Heart

You can probably sense that Jesus wants more than our public performance; he wants our hearts. We want to reduce following

Jesus to a handful of big rules because that feels like it's something we can control. So we say things like, "There is nothing wrong with looking as long as I do not touch. I am not committing adultery." That's exactly what they were doing in Jesus's day, but in the Sermon on the Mount, he raises the standard.

Jesus knows if he has our heart, we can live in freedom. This is true in all areas of our lives. If Jesus does not have your heart, if you try to follow the big rules of religion, you will fail, and immorality will leave you broken. Often you then blame God for the mess you created.

One of the contributing factors to my porn issue early in marriage was the bad counsel I received. Tina and I went through pre-marriage counseling, where we were told by a pastor and counselor that if our sex life got boring, porn could "spice" it up. What a horrible thing to tell a young couple!

Porn (and lust) do not improve your sex life or strengthen your relationship.

Porn (and lust) turn your sex life into a performance and your relationship into a transaction.

Purity begins with the eyes. Jesus says anyone who even *looks at a woman with lust* has committed adultery with her in his heart. We live in an image-driven culture, which means we have to be careful what we see; we have to guard our eyes.

If you want a clean heart, you have to guard your eyes. I cannot consume trash and stay clean. First Corinthians 15:32-33 says, "'Let's feast and drink, for tomorrow we die!' Don't be fooled by those who say such things, for bad company corrupts good character."

Sometimes we are keeping company, on our phone or computer or TV, with people who are *corrupting our good character.* Jesus takes this very seriously. In Matthew 6:22-23 he says, "The eye is the lamp of the body; so then if your eye is clear, your whole body will be full of light. But if your eye is bad, your whole body will be full of darkness. If then the light that is in you is darkness, how great is the darkness!"

Jesus says what we see determines the condition of our souls, and if we are not careful, we will call darkness light. When we begin to call darkness light, we are blind.

What do we do about this? Jesus says, "Pluck it out!"

This is a radical statement, but it was Jesus's way of saying *do whatever you have to do*. When Tina caught me looking at porn on the computer, I unplugged it and threw it in the trash. I did not own a computer *for 10 years.*

It was a radical but important step for my freedom.

Even today my computer, phone, and television are all protected. I want to be careful not to even give myself the opportunity to do the wrong thing. In Proverbs 4:23 Solomon says, "Guard your heart for out of it flow the issues of life."

Spiritual condition drives behavior, and Jesus is pointing out a progression. What begins in our eyes (what we see and think) will soon be in our hands (what we act upon and do). If we do not win the battle with our eyes and for our mind, we do not stand a chance once the problem is in our hands.

We have to win the battle for purity when the battle is winnable.

If I fight the battle when it is still a look or a thought, I can win. James says it this way, "When sin is allowed to grow, it gives birth to death." (James 1:15) Sin will always cost you far more than you intend to pay.

At the risk of sounding like a broken record, the secret to your freedom is *strengthening your relationship with God and other*

Christians. As long as we live in loneliness and isolation, we cannot live in freedom. It is only when we are rightly connected to God and each other that we find sufficient motivation, delight, and relational support to overcome addiction.

When I was in my crisis, marriage failing and fighting addiction, God did not zap me into freedom. A pastor did not pray away my problems. Instead, I experienced a *community of believers* who offered me grace and spoke the truth.

Grace is the most important doctrine in the world. Grace is what separates Christianity from every other religion. Every other religion is like a ladder, a set of rules, works, or a system that claims to be the pathway to God. If you work hard enough or perform well enough, *maybe* God will accept you. Maybe people will accept you. This is why religion creates insecurity, fear, shame, and hiding. Religion produces a false change.

Grace is the opposite.

It is undeserved blessing, unearned love, unconditional acceptance. It is not dependent on the quality of your character or performance but on the richness of God's character. Think back on your life. The people who have had the biggest impact are generally those who showed you grace when you failed. They loved you when you were down and helped you after you messed up.

This is certainly true of my life. It was teachers, coaches, neighbors, church members, and family who were gracious when it would have been easy to give up on me. In third grade, Mrs. Pidgeon showed me grace. In eighth grade it was Mr. Lewis. When I dropped out of seminary and my marriage was failing, Dr. Bennett showed me grace. When I wasn't sure if I had what it takes to be a pastor, Jim Snyder showed me grace.

There have been so many times in my pursuit of purity, if it were not for grace, I would have quit. I would have given up, and the course of my life would have been dramatically altered. Each time, someone showed me grace. Someone who knew my secrets offered me unconditional love. I certainly did not deserve it, yet in that moment I felt loved, heard, and understood.

This empowered me to come out of hiding, be authentic, and find the courage to try again. Everyone needs a safe place to be transparent and vulnerable about their struggles without the fear of rejection. You can't pursue purity alone.

Who is your safe place?

Who knows your secrets?

Who can speak the truth to you?

Dr. Bennett was gracious, but he was also *in my business*. At times it was painful, but I am grateful God brought a man into my life who loved and *corrected* me.

He taught me how to dress, talk, be self-disciplined, write, lead my wife, and preach.

He was constantly saying *don't do that, do this instead*. But he was also constantly saying, *I love you. You have something special. God is going to do something incredible with your life.* He saw all of me—the good parts and the bad parts—and loved me anyway. It allowed me to receive the truth.

And pursuing purity always requires facing up to the truth.

We must love people where they are, but we must love them too much to leave them there.

That's what people did for me, and that's what I hope you will do for the people in your life.

If purity is a struggle you are dealing with, Jesus says it can be overcome.

The first step is to strengthen your relationship with God. He loves you—no matter what—and desires to walk with you. Second, surround yourself with people you trust who will love you, hold you accountable, and speak truth.

We are created for relationships, so when we live in isolation, we become much more vulnerable to destructive behaviors that attempt to medicate our emotional pain. When our relationship with God and our relationships with each other are healthy and flourishing, we rarely choose to remain in destructive patterns.

Pursuing purity takes time because people rarely change overnight. When I look at my life, I am amazed at how much God has changed me. I can see the power of grace and truth at work in my life. I am also amazed that it has taken so long.

Be patient, but be purposeful.

The other side of purity is worth the pursuit.

CHAPTER THIRTEEN

Be Faithful

Enjoy a Great Marriage

I will never forget the night my dad walked out on us. That night has vividly stayed etched in my mind like a scene from a motion picture. The sound of my mom's sobs still echo in my ears; I can see the shiny tracks the tears left as they quietly slid down her cheeks.

She was on the couch, and I was standing like a soldier beside her.

I was only five years old, but somehow I knew my world was about to change.

Dad was standing at the door. He was on the way out and would never return.

It has been more than 40 years, but my mom, my sister, and I are *still* dealing with the consequences of that selfish act today. It's no surprise, because selfishness destroys relationships. In a marriage, selfishness is like cancer. We may have survived the illness, but the side-effects still remain.

Our culture works hard to make us selfish, not that we really need any help. Think about it. We are now the "selfie" culture. Selfies are the most common form of photography. Millennials will take more than 25,000 *selfies* in their lifetime. I guess this dates me, but when they started putting cameras on phones I thought, who wants a camera in their phone? Apparently everyone. My phone now has a camera with three different lenses. Here are some crazy statistics: 74% of Snapchat photos are selfies. 1000 selfies are posted on Instagram every second. In 2015, more people died from taking selfies than from shark attacks! It's no surprise that we have a selfishness problem; we've created a generation of people who think they should be the center of the universe.

There is perhaps no place where this selfishness is more devastating than in marriage.

Selfishness destroys marriages. In a strategically placed two verses, nestled between his words on lust and his words on vows, in Matthew 5:31-32, Jesus said, "You have heard it said, 'Anyone who divorces his wife must give her a certificate of divorce.' But I tell you that anyone who divorces his wife, except for sexual immorality, makes her the victim of adultery, and anyone who marries a divorced woman commits adultery."

To what is Jesus referencing?

Once again, the Jews were keeping the *letter* of the law (the rules) while trampling on the *spirit* of the law. Deuteronomy 24:1 is the law pertaining to marriage and divorce: "When a man takes a wife and marries her, and it happens that she finds no favor in his eyes because he has found some indecency (ervah) in her, and he writes her a certificate of divorce and puts it in her hand and sends her out from his house..."

This verse provided the legal cover for the men of Hebrew society to divorce their wives.

But it was far from what God had intended for the union between husband and wife.

The Hebrew word *ervah*, translated "some indecency", literally means "nakedness." In rabbinical teaching, *ervah* refers to a forbidden sexual relationship from the biblical expression, "to uncover nakedness". This is used often in Leviticus chapters 18 and 20 to condemn immoral sexual practices. This is important because this phrase *limits* the acceptable reasons for divorce and confirms that the sexual practices condemned in Leviticus 18 and 20 are part of the moral law and therefore have carried over into the New Testament.

Jesus is reaffirming the high standard of sexual morality and the importance and permanence of marriage. In America, marriage is no longer as valued or honored as it once was. Today, fewer adults are getting married, and when they do decide to marry, it is later than ever. Why are so many so unsure about marriage? It may be because of bad information. We have all heard the marriage and divorce statistic that 50% of marriages end in divorce. But is that true? Shaunti Feldhahn, in her book *The Good News About Marriage*, uncovers the truth about marriage in America. After years of research, she discovered that the divorce rate in America has never been close to 50%. The divorce rate for first marriages is actually between 20-25 percent depending on which study you read. Not only that, but 80% of married couples report being *happy*. That's really good news! We have also been told that the divorce rate in the church is not any better. Actually, the divorce rate is 27% lower for couples who attend church regularly together.

Most divorces are not usually caused by some big insurmountable problem, but by small, common issues left unaddressed. Most people go into marriage assuming it will be easy. After all, if we love each other, if she or he is "the one", then a lifetime together should be easy, right?

I have been a pastor now for twenty-two years, and I do not know a married couple married longer than a week who think marriage is easy. As my mentor used to say, "Love is intoxicating, but marriage will sober you up."

Think about it this way; in Genesis 2, Adam and Eve are in the Garden of Eden. They are living with God, enjoying the garden without kids, with all they could ever need. One chapter later, they are ready to file for divorce!

The act of marriage is not easy, but it is incredibly good.

Marriage is hard work, but it is worth it. Marriage teaches us how to build intimacy with another person and with God. In fact, typically the issues we have with our spouse are similar or identical to the issues we have with God. Marriage, more than anything else, has forced me to learn maturity and taught me how to do relationships well.

Here are five practical ways to protect your marriage:

- **Prioritize your marriage.** Make a decision that marriage is a battle you will win! When I look back over my twenty-four years of marriage, I can see a direct correlation to what is good, mature, and strong in me.

My marriage has done more to expose my character and maturity issues and force me to grow up than any other relationship or situation. This "crisis" creates ongoing opportunities for me to learn and grow. As I learn and grow, my maturity helps me in every other area of my life. I cannot think of one accomplishment that can possibly produce as much happiness in your life as a great marriage.

You may be chasing a mirage and sacrificing what is closest to you. No matter what you accomplish or acquire, if you blow your family up, the day will come when you will regret the sacrifice and the choice you made.

Honor your commitment and fight for your marriage. It's a battle you'll be glad to win.

- **Keep working on your marriage.** There is no finish line, just continual progress. Tina and I are still working to strengthen our marriage. We went on a marriage retreat this fall; we read books together, and we regularly talk about the condition of our relationship. We want to intentionally invest in our love for each other. We are constantly growing in our capacity to understand each other, to process conflict, to love and serve each other, to appreciate our differences, and to build our future together. This is intentional. It is fun and encouraging when you see your relationship moving in a good direction. Little improvements make a big difference. Never stop working on yourself so you never stop working on your marriage.

- **Master conflict.** If you figure out how to handle conflict, you can handle anything that comes up in your marriage. Most couples are terrible at conflict. Some attack each other, and some avoid conflict. Neither way is healthy. Avoiding the issues means you have a growing list of unresolved grievances. Eventually, this will blow up, and the collateral damage can be devastating.

Remember, conflict is not bad.

Conflict actually has the power to improve your relationship. Conflict simply means we have an issue in our relationship that is causing it to weaken. Understanding that and resolving it strengthens your relationship. When conflict happens, you must remember, *you are on the same team.* This is critical.

Never attack your spouse! In your marriage, your spouse is all you have. Do not think of your spouse as the problem. Your spouse is the solution. If you attack the only other person in your marriage relationship, how can you hope to resolve your issues? You are on the same team, so commit to working together to overcome the challenges you will inevitably face throughout your life.

When conflict happens, and you remember you are on the same team, you can work together to find a win-win solution. In conflict, we usually think someone is going to win and someone is going to lose, but that is a mistake. Marriage isn't 50/50; it's 100/100. You either both win, or you both lose. When Tina and I experience conflict, meaning when what she wants and what I want diverge, we can almost always create a win-win solution if we keep the end goal in mind. We can almost always figure out a way for her to get what she wants and for me to get what I want. In fact, I cannot think of a time when that was not true. Work to come up with a win-win solution.

Finally, when conflict does happen (and it will), don't hold grudges; make up! This means if you say or do the wrong thing, do not make excuses, do not be a victim, do not find someone to blame— just take responsibility. Your spouse knows you aren't perfect. They aren't expecting perfection; they are expecting authenticity and accountability. When I do something dumb, I admit it; I ask for forgiveness, and I try to learn from my mistake. If we both do this, we constantly grow in our capacity to love each other.

- **Create and protect your financial margin.** The number-one cause of divorce is financial stress. Fortunately, this is something you can control. Be very careful about overextending yourself financially. The world says if you just had more you would be happy. If you are not happy, nothing that money can buy—a house, a car, an outfit, a trip—will make you happy. If you get overextended financially and destroy your marriage, then lose half of all you have in divorce, you will be broke, unhappy, and alone. You have to find your happiness, the blessing we've been talking about, in your relationship with Jesus and people. This empowers you to make wise financial decisions which protect your family and your happiness.

- **Find your satisfaction in Jesus, and love your spouse.** Many people expect their spouse to make them happy. This is a totally unrealistic and misplaced expectation. That means you are worshipping your spouse. I cannot trust Tina for my happiness, security, and identity. I must find that in Jesus so I can love my spouse and other people. If I do not settle this in my relationship with Jesus, I will use people rather than love them. This again is what the first part of the Beatitudes was all about.

When it comes to marriage, Jesus wants us to do more than simply keep the legal requirements of the union. He wants us to live out our marriage commitments, love our spouse selflessly, serve them humbly, and work together to impact the world for his glory.

When you do this, there is no sweeter relationship this side of heaven.

CHAPTER FOURTEEN

Be Truthful

Keep Your Vows

It was 1989—31 years ago. I was a 17-year old boy, standing in a hospital at the bedside of my dying grandfather. He was a great man, a great pastor, and a respected leader all across eastern North Carolina. Now, he was on the edge of eternity, about to cross the threshold we will all one day walk across.

That night, just before he died, he laid his hands on my shoulders and prayed that his ministry mantle would fall on me. When he finished praying, he took a breath and looked into my eyes and said these words: "Be a man of integrity, be honest, and be a man of your word." His name was Sam Whichard, and I will never forget those words and how powerfully they've shaped my life.

We live in a culture where the truth is hard to find.

In 2017, *Collins Dictionary* declared "Fake News" the word of the year.

University of Massachusetts psychologist Robert S. Feldman wrote in the *Journal of Basic and Applied Social Psychology*, that 60 percent of people lie at least once, but an average of two to three times, during a 10-minute conversation.

The truth is (pun intended) we have gotten pretty comfortable with lying. Here are some common lies we tell without missing a blink. Have you ever used these lies?

- "On my way!"
- "It must have gone to my spam folder."
- "My phone died."
- "I forgot."
- "I'm fine."
- "The traffic was terrible!"
- "I have been totally slammed!"
- "Let's get together soon."
- "It's great to see you!"
- "Just kidding."
- "That looks great on you."
- "I'm praying for you."
- "Your baby is adorable."

It feels like there needs to be an emoji next to each one just to convey the true message. Or an explanation for what we're *really* thinking but are too afraid to say.

Lying has always been a problem; it is just getting increasingly easy to get caught. For most of human history, when you said something it immediately disappeared. There was no record of what you said. But written language and technology have changed that. Today when we say something by text, email, on social media, on camera, or even on a phone call, that conversation is recorded. Often there is a permanent record of everything we say, and in the future, it has the potential to affect everything we do.

Needless to say, the truth is becoming more and more important.

It's also becoming more and more fleeting.

This begs the question: *why do we lie?* Sometimes our lying is a legitimate attempt to be nice or to protect a person's feelings. It would not be nice to go around being painfully honest with people about stuff that does not matter. Telling a person that they look older, heavier, tired, and more wrinkled would not be helpful or well-received.

Sometimes our lying is fear-driven and compounded by our fear of rejection. We want people to like us, so we lie to cover our imperfections and make ourselves look better to gain acceptance. Sometimes our lying is intentionally deceptive to influence people, to gain an unfair advantage, or to manipulate them into doing what they would not do if they knew the truth.

Deep down, we know this is manipulative, but we can't seem to help ourselves.

So what does Jesus have to say about honesty?

In the Old Testament, you would make a promise by swearing and bring God's name into the promise. This was serious business, so your oath better be the truth, and you better do what you said. In other words, you needed to be willing to do whatever it took to fulfill your vow.

By the time Jesus entered the scene, the Pharisees created a loophole. Surprise, surprise.

They would deceive people into thinking they were pious and holy by swearing "by heaven" or "by God's creation" or "by Jerusalem" or "by the Holy Temple". However, the Pharisees *only* considered it binding if you included God's name or if you swore by the gold in the temple. It was kind of like crossing your fingers behind your back when you were a kid. This gave them an out which they used to great advantage. They would swear an oath but then deceive (and dishearten) people when they failed to keep their vows. It's little wonder they weren't liked or trusted.

Today we say things like, "I swear on my momma's grave!" or "I swear to God."

Jesus says stop.

Stop all the swearing, and just do what you say.

If we are being truthful, there is no need to swear by anything at all.

Why is Jesus so concerned about the truth?

First, truth requires honesty, and honesty is the fiber that strengthens our relationships. Trust is the foundation for any relationship; lying erodes trust. If the blessing we desire flows through our relationships, then we need to attack anything that attacks our relationships—that includes a lack of truth.

Jesus said, "You will know the truth, and the truth will set you free" (John 8:32).

Truth protects our relationships and our freedom. Jesus went on to say, "You are the children of your father the devil, and you love to do the evil things he does. He was a murderer from the beginning. He has always hated the truth because there is no truth in him. When he lies, it is consistent with his character; for he is a liar and the father of lies" (John 8:44).

Lies destroy relationships. That's why Satan deceived Eve with a lie and destroyed the relationship between God and others (Adam). "You won't die!" the serpent replied to the woman. "God knows that your eyes will be opened as soon as you eat it, and you will be like God, knowing both good and evil" (Genesis 3:4-5).

This one lie destroyed man's relationship with God and Adam and Eve's relationship with each other (Genesis 3). Its consequences were felt throughout the Old Testament. Abraham lied about Sarah being his wife (Genesis 20). Jacob lied to his father and claimed to be Esau (Genesis 27). Laban lied to Jacob and gave him Leah instead of Rachel (Genesis 29). Joseph's brothers sold Joseph into slavery and lied about it to their father (Genesis 37).

In each of these examples, dishonesty weakened or destroyed the relationship.

Honesty, on the other hand, strengthens relationships and accelerates your spiritual growth. One of the most common ways we are dishonest and stunt our growth is our unwillingness (even in the church) to admit we are struggling. We have a tendency to hide our pain and hide our sin. This stifles our growth.

Everyone has to make a decision: Am I going to be dishonest and hide, or am I going to be honest and grow? If you hide your pain or your sin, you will remain stuck in it. If you come out of hiding, become honest about your pain and your struggles, God will heal your pain and set you free. James says it this way, "Confess your sins to each other and pray for each other so that you may be healed" (James 5:16). You may be thinking, *I don't know if I can be honest and share my struggles. What would people think?*

I get it.

Vulnerability is a scary step, but I am more afraid of living with secrets and destroying my relationships than worrying about what people think. I am more afraid of explaining to my wife, my kids, or to you that I did something stupid after my secrets come out than I am about admitting I'm struggling now. I am more afraid of hurting the people I love the most than I am of being judged for being imperfect. (Spoiler alert: they know you aren't perfect already.)

Over the last few years, I have had many pastor friends who have blown it. There is one thing they all have one common—secrets! I have weaknesses, and I feel tempted just like anyone else. God is still working on me. However, I just talk about it with Tina, with my team, and with my congregation.

When I am honest and transparent, it allows me to learn and grow.

When I remain in hiding, I get stuck in my sin.

We hide and are afraid because we fear rejection. We think that if everyone knew the truth about us, they would not love us anymore. This is what is great about the gospel and one of the distinguishing characteristics of Christianity—*God already knows everything about you.* God knows all your secrets, and yet He loves you enough that He was willing to give up His only Son to have an eternal relationship with you.

He wants us to love each other the same way.

To be sure, we often shoot our own wounded, but one thing that should characterize every Christian is grace. This starts with you. You can't control what others do or how they react to someone who is hurting and broken; you can control yourself and whether or not you react in love.

In Galatians 6:1-3 Paul writes,

Dear brothers and sisters, if another believer is overcome by some sin, you who are godly should gently and humbly help that person back onto the right path. And be careful not to fall into the same temptation yourself. Share each other's burdens, and in this way obey the law of Christ. If you think you are too important to help someone, you are only fooling yourself. You are not that important.

This verse reminds us that we all have issues. If you do not think you have issues, *that* is your issue! The church must be a place of grace. The church should be like a gym. When we discover a weakness in our body, we talk to our trainer about that weakness and then work on it *together*.

When we have a character issue, a relational issue, or a leadership issue, we should feel the freedom to talk about it and then work on it together. Plus, we are called to reach people who are far away from God, who are imperfect, and who have issues. That was certainly true for you before you experienced the saving grace of God.

We must love people where they are, but we must love them too much to leave them there. Paul says if you are mature, come alongside those who have lost their way and help them get back on the right path. The spiritual are trainers who should come alongside and help others build their relationship with God and people so they can experience a blessed life!

People have done this with me over and over again, and it has changed my life.

Honesty also strengthens our witness. I love the honesty and transparency of Paul. Paul says, "This is a trustworthy saying, and everyone should accept it: Christ Jesus came into the world to save sinners—and I am the worst of them all. But God had mercy on me so that Christ Jesus could use me as *a prime example of his great patience with even the worst sinners*. Then others will realize that they, too, can believe in him and receive eternal life" (1 Timothy 1:15-17). [Emphasis mine]

Paul knew he had his flaws.

His sins and self-righteousness resulted in the death of many early Christians.

To his credit, he owns it and uses *everything* (even the most humiliating parts of his past) to point people to Jesus. He knew that everyone who looked at his life couldn't help but realize, *if God could use Paul, He can use me.*

How honest are you about your journey of faith?

My grandfather gave me a charge to be a man of integrity, honesty, and a man of my word. I've done my best to honor that charge— even when it hurts. The number-one compliment I get about my preaching is my transparency. Why? Because when I talk about my struggles and what God has done in me, it gives people hope.

The same can be true for you. Your honesty strengthens your witness and is fuel for growth—both for you and the people who are watching you.

CHAPTER FIFTEEN

Be Bigger

Love Your Enemies

E nemy is an interesting word. It's a strong word. Most of us probably hear that word and think, sure, there are people I don't like, but *I don't really have any enemies.* After all, enemies are what we read about in books or watch in the movies. Enemies are bad guys who are armed to the teeth and willing to do anything to stop you. When we think of enemies like that, it's hard to relate.

So why does Jesus use that word in the Sermon on the Mount? Did he know something we didn't?

Flash forward to today, and think about the level of anger and bitterness and animosity that you encounter when you get online or open Twitter or Facebook on your phone. From that perspective, you'd be hard-pressed to find anyone who *isn't* someone else's enemy.

Jesus may not have had social media in mind, but he knew something about the human heart. Six times Jesus said *you have heard the law that says...* This phrase is like the teacher calling on you in class when they know you didn't do your homework. You can almost see the Pharisees start to squirm. In each of those six cases, they had been trying to manipulate God's law to justify their anger, lust, abuse, oppression of women, dishonesty, and violence.

Each time Jesus destroys their loophole, raises the moral standard, and promises to provide what we need to live this new, blessed life. He knew that to usher in the Kingdom of God, his children needed to live by a higher standard. In this kingdom, there was a higher ethic, the ethic of love.

Rules always have loopholes, and our nature is to find and exploit that loophole.

Jesus wants more for us. He wants love. When love fills our hearts, it takes over and compels us to treat people the way Jesus did. In order to drive this point home, Jesus gets into our business. He invades our personal space because that's where he can find our hearts.

In Matthew 5:44 he says, "Love your enemies and pray for those who persecute you."

We know how hard those words are to hear today. Think about how it would have been for Jesus's audience. Their enemies of the day looked and acted like enemies. The Romans were armed to the teeth. They could crucify you if they wanted to and often did. They were Gentiles who didn't believe in the Jewish faith. Worst of all, they were oppressors in every sense of the word.

The Jews assumed the Messiah would come and destroy the Romans. In fact, Jews were waiting in the wings, anxiously anticipating the kind of Messiah who would put the Romans in their place. This made Jesus's words confusing; in their minds, the last thing the Messiah would say is to *love* them.

Even today, most people read the words of the Old Testament and totally misunderstand and mischaracterize the heart of God. I was with a young pastor recently who said he was so thankful for the

God of the New Testament and so thankful for grace. I understood what he meant, but there is one God. He spans the entire Bible, and He does not change!

God is not more gracious today than He was in the Old Testament. In the Old Testament, God was undeniably patient and long-suffering but His love for the innocent compels Him to judge the guilty in order to restrain sin and its painful consequences. To Moses in Exodus 34:6-7 God speaks: "The Lord! The God of compassion and mercy. I am slow to anger and filled with unfailing love and faithfulness. I lavish love to a thousand generations. I forgive iniquity, rebellion, and sin."

Jesus came to change our hearts. He came so that we might become more like the Father and point people (even our enemies) to Him. That's why he issues the higher directive to *love your enemies*.

It's easy to love people we like, who think like we do, and do things that make us happy.

That's no big sacrifice.

Thank God He doesn't love that way, or none of us would be loved!

Love imitates God. Jesus says when we love, we are acting like our Father in heaven.

When we love, we imitate God. God loves His enemies. God loves the people we hate.

Love always requires freedom. That's why bad things sometimes happen in the world. When God created the world, it was perfect and sinless—it was literally heaven on earth. Genesis 1:1 says, "In the beginning, God created the heavens and the earth. Heaven and earth were together. God and man were together."

It was a world without the sin, sickness, disease, pain, or suffering of any kind that plagues us today. However, because God loves us, He created us with the freedom to reject Him.

When God created man, He had three options.

First, He could force us to obey. That is not love; it is coercion.

Second, God could kill us if we did not obey. That is not love; it is murder.

Adam and Eve decided to reject God and to declare their independence. This introduced sin, death, pain, and suffering into God's good creation.

This led to the third option, one that would come at great cost—God could create us, set us free, and win our love. That is the essence of love.

The Bible is the story of God working throughout redemptive history to demonstrate His love to win our hearts. When Jesus said to *love your enemies,* he wasn't speaking lightly. He knew the price he himself would have to pay to demonstrate that love. He offered his own life as a demonstration of his Father's love in order to transform our hearts through faith.

The God of the Old Testament and the New Testament patiently endures sin and the pain and suffering sin has caused in order to *give us all* a chance to understand the gospel and turn to Him in faith.

God is love, and He rewards us when we love others.

That's an interesting thought that makes loving those who are difficult to love just a little easier to do. In verse 46, Jesus asks the rhetorical question, *If you only love those who love you, what reward is there?* That's reciprocal love, not transformational love.

Compare that to loving your enemies. What does that kind of love say to the person who is difficult to love? When we love our enemies, we are rewarded by God. In the church world, sometimes we feel bad about doing things for a reward. However, it appears God has wired us to be motivated by rewards and that God enjoys rewarding us.

Living the Christian life is a sacrifice.

We are not living for ourselves, for our glory, for our comfort, or for this moment.

We are living for the glory of God.

How can I live and love this way? Jesus knew that there was not a law that would ever make you love. The only way we will love as Jesus loves is if we grow in our understanding of his love for us. As we understand how much he loves us, his love fills our hearts with love for God and love for people.

This love enables us to serve others.

Again, this is why we must be with Jesus—so that we can become like Jesus; then we can do what Jesus did and love our enemies. If you are serious about becoming like Jesus and experiencing the blessing, then you must get serious about loving others. We seem to be more divided than ever, yet love is the one thing that every person needs. It's the one thing that can bring us together.

Jesus sets a high standard in Matthew 5:48, "Be perfect, therefore, as your heavenly Father is perfect." We gain this perfection, not by managing our behavior but by getting close to Jesus and allowing him to change our hearts. Then we can love when we don't feel like it or when the other person is prickly and unlovable. We love when people vote differently than we do or have beliefs we don't necessarily agree with. We love when we're tired, or hurting, or sad. We love when it costs us something and remember that is how Jesus loved us.

At the end of the day, we love because God has filled our hearts with His love!

CHAPTER SIXTEEN

Be Generous

Give Freely

There's an anecdotal story about American billionaire John D. Rockefeller that you've probably heard before. In his prime, Rockefeller was the richest man in the world. He was America's first billionaire, and his wealth was equivalent to nearly 2% of America's GDP.

To put that into perspective, the U.S. gross domestic product in 2018 was $21.44 trillion dollars. That's $21,440,000,000,000. Two percent of that number is north of $428 *billion* dollars. The richest man in the world today, Amazon founder Jeff Bezos, is worth less than half of that.

John D. Rockefeller was loaded.

Through his company, Standard Oil, he amassed a fortune the likes of which the world had never seen. So what's the anecdotal story? Someone once asked John Davison Rockefeller, Sr., the richest man in the world, *how much is enough?*

His answer: "Just a little more."

By all accounts, Rockefeller used large portions of his fortune for good. He made donations to education that helped start colleges. He helped fund the Rockefeller Institute for Medical Research and the Rockefeller Foundation. His only son carried on his legacy and was instrumental in helping establish the United Service Organization (USO) and donated the land in New York City where the United Nations headquarters resides.

There's no doubt that having money opens up doors. But regardless of how much or how little money you have, one thing is true—money is something that can hold a great deal of influence over our lives if we aren't careful. Jesus understood how we handle our money has a huge impact on the condition of our souls. In fact, in one of his final teachings, just before heading to Jerusalem where he would offer his life on the cross for us, he sits his disciples down and warns them not to idolize money but to invest it in the kingdom.

Deep down, we know money doesn't make us happy, but far too many of us live like it is the most critical thing in the world. We work in jobs we don't like, buy things we don't need, dream about stuff we want to get, and generally are miserable because of money.

It shouldn't be this way.

There are three lies we often believe about money.

The first is that having more will make you secure. Money is really nothing more than a promise. It's ink printed on fine linen paper. It's only as good as the government that backs it, and it can be lost (or made) in the blink of an eye. Steve Jobs, one of the wealthiest men in the world, died of cancer at fifty-six years old. He had more money than he needed, but it still couldn't save him. If you put your faith in money, one day you'll realize that it's a good servant but a lousy master.

The second lie we believe about money is that what you have defines who you are. It's easy to catch a case of the comparison blues. Social media makes it possible now to see how incredible everyone else's life is and how boring yours is by comparison. (Spoiler alert: a picture or a post rarely shows the entire story.) If your stuff defines who you are, then, frankly you're a pretty shallow person. In Luke 12:15, Jesus said, "Beware! Guard against every kind of greed. Life is not measured by how much you own." This was from the man who owned next to nothing, yet left an incredible mark on the world.

The final lie we believe is that our stuff belongs to us. This ties back into our sense of self-worth, primarily when it comes to our jobs. We work hard to get a paycheck every two weeks. We invest and save for our retirement so we can live the good life one day. It can be easy to be filled with pride and consider that your bank account, your house, your cars, your clothes, and anything else you value is your own. The Bible tells a different story. It says we are merely managers (or stewards) of God's stuff. God is the owner. He is the giver of all things.

Jesus knew that each of these lies would be appealing; that's why he spoke about money in the Sermon on the Mount. He opens in Matthew Chapter 6 with teaching on how we should give to others. Then he teaches about prayer and fasting (which we'll cover in the next chapter) before circling back to money specifically. He closes with a section on worry (which we'll cover later).

If you've ever struggled with the stress that money can cause, you can probably see the relationship between giving, praying and fasting, money, worry, and how they all work together. Let's unpack what Jesus says about money and redefine how we think.

There's a sales technique that marketers have used for years: when you pitch people to buy something, you don't refer to the cost or price. Rather, you frame it in terms of *investment*. An investment is something we spend now in hopes of gaining future value.

When Jesus began to teach about giving, he reframed it in light of future investment.

The Pharisees were big on giving—as long as people *saw* them giving. Never ones to miss an opportunity to look holy and righteous, they made seemingly grand gestures to "help" the common people. Jesus says, "So when you give to the needy, do not announce it with trumpets, as the hypocrites do in the synagogues and on the streets, to be honored by men. I tell you the truth, they have received their reward in full.

Jesus redefined giving as an investment not *for* people, but *in* people.

You may not see the fruit of your investment for years, but a good investment yields dividends. The Pharisees were less interested in helping others. They didn't care about the people; needy people were just a means to an end. Giving made them look good.

The whole message of the Sermon on the Mount was upside-down, redefined thinking. Jesus was more concerned with the *recipient* of the gift than the audacity of the giver. He knew that giving, investing in the life of another should change your heart as well.

His way: give in secret, or "do not let your left hand know what your right is doing."

When you learn to give this way, guess who you impress?

The Father.

God sees both your gift and your heart. When those two align, your investment in others is multiplied, and the fruit it bears is shown in you. The law says give a certain amount and make sure everyone knows it. Jesus says nothing is more valuable than people.

When we give in love, we invest in others.

Giving is also an investment in our relationship with God.

When Jesus circles back to money, his tone intensifies. He reminds us that all our stuff, the things we store up here on earth, stay here. They don't come with us when we die. They fall apart, break, and fade away.

Then he drops the bomb: *Where your treasure is, there your heart will be also.*

If you are a practicing Christian, you want your love for God to increase. That's why you get up and go to church on Sunday morning. It's why you read your Bible, meditate on scripture, and pray each day. Most Christians do their best to put God first in most areas of our lives.

This should include our money. Jesus knew that money had the power to either move you closer to God or move you further away. "No one can serve two masters. Either he will hate one and love the other, or he will be devoted to one and despise the other. You cannot serve both God and Money (Matthew 6:24).

This is one reason tithing is so powerful. When you give to God first, you reset your heart. You make Him the priority. You invest in His Kingdom and equip Him to do the work. God doesn't need your $10, $100, or $1,000 as the offering plate passes by. He's the creator and owner of everything. However, He does want your heart, and He knows that if you are giving first, then He won't have to compete with money.

The story of Cain and Abel provides a good illustration of how giving is all about relationships. In Genesis 4:1-7 we see that Abel gave his first and his best. He worshiped God, so it was no sacrifice to give out of love. Cain was religious, and giving was an obligation. He gave God *some*, but not his best, and certainly not willingly. He fulfilled the letter of the law but neglected the spirit.

And when his heart drifted far enough from God, he ultimately killed his brother.

You have a decision to make: do you want to give God first place?

When you want God to be first, you give Him the first of your day, the first of your week, the first of your time, the first of your heart, and the first of your money. We do not give to help God out. We give to guard our hearts against idolatry and materialism. We are His children, and every good parent wants the best for the heart of their child. God is no different.

Jesus urges us to keep an eye on those things we spend our money on. Have you ever noticed how you keep an eye on the things you have invested the most in? Whether it's relationships, sports, our career, or our money—what captivates our attention holds our hearts.

Giving is an investment in our relationship with God. Every time you give, you are saying, *God, I love you, and you are first in my life*. When God is in first place, every other thing lines up in the right place.

When Jesus hiked up the Mount of Olives and began delivering the Sermon on the Mount, he was planting his flag in the ground and declaring the message that God's Kingdom was here. He knew that his words would get people's attention, and ultimately he'd pay with his life.

But the Kingdom was worth the sacrifice.

When you give, you are investing in God's kingdom.

Jesus says, "Do not store up yourselves treasures on earth... store up your treasure in heaven" (Matthew 6:19-20). We all have a little bit of desire for instant gratification. We shop and expect things delivered within two days; we stream movies and shows "on-demand"; we want our food to be delivered hot, fresh, and quickly when we sit down in a restaurant.

But kingdom-building takes time.

When we invest in our 401k, we do so knowing we won't see the results for decades.

When we give to God's kingdom, we may not see the results this side of heaven. That forces us to choose—are we only interested in what we can see, or do we trust God with everything we can't see?

When we give, we are building God's *eternal* kingdom; we are growing God's *immediate* family, and that is an eternal investment. It takes time. It takes discipline. But it yields the best results.

When we put God first, it empowers us to manage the rest.

When something else is first, it's never enough.

God wants to bless us. He wants to take what we give and use it to invest in people. When we invest in our relationship with Jesus, we invest in his Kingdom. But the truth is, the benefit pours back on us. Giving blesses us. In 1 Corinthians 9: 6-8, Paul writes:

Remember this: Whoever sows sparingly will also reap sparingly, and whoever sows generously will also reap generously. Each of you should give what you have decided in your heart to give, not reluctantly or under compulsion, for God loves a cheerful giver. And God is able to bless you abundantly, so that in all things at all times, having all that you need, you will abound in every good work.

You will never regret generosity. It's an investment in others that pays you dividends. Put money in its proper place. Give to God first, and ask Him to help you manage the rest.

Focus on kingdom-building and creating treasures that last.

One day, you'll see the returns on your investments and be amazed at what God has done.

CHAPTER SEVENTEEN

Be Connected

Pray Powerfully

Recently, I invited a group of new friends to join me for a Bible study built around the Starting Point curriculum by North Point Ministries. This curriculum was designed for people with questions and doubts about faith to have a "starting point" to discuss matters of deep importance.

We opened up by spending some time talking about prayer. One guy explained that in his past experience, "prayer time" had been a real turn off. He said it seemed like everyone was either trying to have the most dramatic prayer request story to share, or the prayer requests were about trivial issues like a pet or a minor illness. He didn't like how when people prayed they said *God* or *Father God* over and over again.

To him, it all seemed phony, religious, and impersonal.

I understand what he's saying, but here's the thing—Jesus is personal, and prayer is simply talking and listening to God.

Jesus describes prayer as a relational tool that strengthens our relationships with God and each other. To some, God is impersonal, distant, and far away. They may believe that there is a creator, but they can't see Him as someone who actually knows them and cares about them.

But God *did* create you to *know* you. He also wants to share His life with you.

That is what prayer is all about.

Prayer is about *cultivating* our relationship with God. Just as a garden needs cultivation to grow, a relationship needs conversation to grow. It's impossible to begin or strengthen a relationship without communication. In the silence, you'd stand there and look at one another until you got bored and walked away.

Prayer is our ongoing conversation with God, and no matter how silent we are, He's always there waiting to listen and speak to us.

For the disciples, this was a totally new concept. They had seen firsthand how Jesus often broke away to quiet places to spend time in prayer with the Father. This type of intimate conversation was far different than the public, wordy prayers of the Pharisees.

The disciples yearned for this connection to the Father so when Jesus modeled a prayer, it gave them (and us) everything we needed to connect with God. The verses in Matthew 6:9-13 are often called the Lord's Prayer. Although you may have it memorized, it is not necessarily a prayer to recite, although there is nothing wrong with that. Rather, the Lord's Prayer is a *model* or a formula for a prayer that allows you to speak deeply and intimately with the Father.

This, then, is how you should pray: 'Our Father in heaven, hallowed be your name, your kingdom come, your will be done, on earth as it is in heaven. Give us today our daily bread. And forgive us our debts, as we also have forgiven our debtors. And lead us not into temptation, but deliver us from the evil one.'

This prayer is simple and powerful. And like the rest of Jesus's teaching, what he does with the minimal amount of words speaks volumes about how best to live.

Jesus redefines prayer in a way that makes it personal, relational, and relevant. When we learn to pray, it's far from phony, religious, and impersonal. Rather, a dynamic prayer life becomes a vital part of a life well-lived. Here is how the Lord's Prayer redefined communication with the Father and cultivates our spiritual growth.

First, *prayer increases your humility*. Notice how Jesus begins— *Our Father.*

Jesus could have said *my* Father but he didn't. Right out of the gate Jesus wants us to remember, we are not alone, life is not all about us, and we are part of a family. In this prayer Jesus prays *our* father, *our* daily bread, and *our* sins.

Our culture is obsessed with self. But when we pray, Jesus does not want us to think only of ourselves. Jesus wants us to consider what is happening in our family. What are others going through? What are their needs? When we learn to pray and think this way it empowers us to *serve each other*.

If we are part of a spiritual family, then we should all seek to serve one another in love. By saying *our* at the start of his prayer, Jesus wanted to teach us to see beyond ourselves, our needs, and our problems. It was how he would live out his ministry. In Matthew 20:28 Jesus said, "the Son of Man came not to be served but to serve…" In Matthew 23:11 Jesus reminds us that "the greatest among you is the servant of all."

When you pray in this way, God will remind you what other people are going through and prompt you to pray for them. This is humility in action.

• *Prayer also builds your trust.*

Trust is built through relationship, and prayer is the link to a sovereign God who longs for a relationship with you. Jesus could have taught us to pray *our God, our Lord, our King,* or *our Sovereign.* God is all of those things and so much more. Instead, Jesus encourages us to speak to God relationally, affectionately, and personally.

Father.

No one in the Old Testament ever addressed God in such casual terms. He was Yahweh, Jehovah, El Shaddai, Elohim, Adonai. Moses had to remove his sandals to stand before the burning bush, Joshua fell on his face in the desert sand when confronted by the Angel of the Lord—Jesus looks up and calls him Father. The message is clear. We do not have to address God as slaves; we address Him as sons and daughters.

There's one important thing here to consider. If God is my Father and wants what's best for me, then why doesn't He answer my prayers? I can use an illustration from my own life. I'm a father, and when my kids ask me for something, the answer is not always yes. When you love someone, sometimes the answer is "no" or "not yet." No child wants to hear this when they are looking for a "yes." However, they usually do not have the same perspective as I do. They cannot see what I can see, so they can't fully understand the decision I'm making.

Since they know me, and we have constant conversations, they know that I love them and want what's best for them. As we talk to God in prayer or trust, our faith begins to grow. The longer the conversation, the more we can look back and see the hand of God at work in our life.

- *Prayer also increases your faith.*

Think about it. In heaven, God is large and in charge. He is the transcendent creator and sustainer of the universe. Psalm 19:1 says, "The heavens declare the glory of God; the skies proclaim the work of His hands." When you look up at the stars you see the handiwork of God. He is all-powerful, all-wise, the King of the Universe.

Yet he longs to talk to you in prayer. Isn't that incredible?

In life, often our problems seem big and our God seems small. Actually, the opposite is true. Our God is big, and our problems are small and temporary. It's only when we pull back from prayer that we get overwhelmed by our problems. They loom large because we don't have the perspective of God to give us clarity.

God wants us to relate to Him like a child. When you were a child and you got a splinter or scrape or broken bone, you ran to your parents because you trusted them to love you and take care of you. They made your big troubles seem small by the comparison of their peace and presence. That is what God wants to do for you now.

Paul (who knew a thing or two about big problems) calls them *light and momentary* troubles in 2 Corinthians 4:17. He had his eyes on God so he could trust Him in times of trouble and worship Him in faith. This is the essence of prayer.

- *Prayer leads us into worship.*

After acknowledging God as Father and recognizing His place in heaven, Jesus says four words: *hallowed be your name.* Names are important because they tell us something about the person. Jesus was recognizing that God's name is to be worshiped and praised. It is the name above all names.

It's important to remember both the familiarity that comes with God being our Father and the holiness that requires His name to be exalted. Both are critical for worship. As a Father, He is approachable. As God, He is worthy of worship.

When we put our focus on God, it produces worship in our hearts. When we put our focus on our problems or other things, we can miss God. Prayer redirects our attention to God, where we see Him in His glory.

- *Prayer allows you to surrender.*

Have you ever just wanted to give up, lie down, and take a rest? We all reach that point eventually. It's tough to strive and struggle and grind and push. Add in a dash of global pandemic, political uncertainty, and social media discord, and it's easy to see why we're exhausted.

Jesus knew this, so he spoke the next part of the Lord's Prayer: *Your kingdom come; Your will be done, on earth as it is in heaven.* The truth is, once we know God and have a relationship with Him, we would never dream of being in charge. Because God is my Father, because I can trust Him, because of His character, power, and wisdom, I want to do whatever He says to do! It's that simple.

Surrender often is, but something in our being wants to hang on as long as possible.

Most people think prayer is about changing the mind of God. How can I get God to do what I want Him to do? That's why people approach it as a wish list or obligation. Actually, prayer is about changing *me*. The goal of prayer is not to convince God to join me but to surrender and decide to join Him. Prayer changes me. It realigns my mind, heart, perspective, priorities, and character. God changes my circumstances primarily by changing me.

This was exhibited nowhere more clearly than when Jesus was praying in the Garden of Gethsemane just before he was betrayed. Matthew 26:39 paints a vivid picture of surrender: "Going a little farther, he fell with his face to the ground and prayed,'My Father, if it is possible, may this cup be taken from me. Yet not as I will, but as You will.'"

Genuine prayer always brings my will into submission to His will. This brings us to the next benefit of prayer.

• *Prayer teaches you to be content.*

Jesus says, *give us this day our daily bread.* Isn't that a wonderful prayer for the day? Lord, just give me what I need for today. Feed me, clothe me, give me peace. Take care of me *just for today.*

It is not a coincidence that this is sandwiched between the two passages about giving and money. We have to be careful not to get so focused on what we are trying to achieve or obtain that we miss God's provision. There is nothing wrong with having money or success as long as the money does not have you. It's a theme we see echoed over and over again.

- Mark 8:36, "What does it profit a man to gain the whole world and yet forfeit his soul."

- Hebrews 13:5, "Be content with what you have. For Jesus said, I will never leave you nor forsake you."

- Proverbs 30:8-9, "... give me neither poverty nor riches! Give me just enough to satisfy my needs."

- 2 Timothy 6:17, "Teach those who are rich in this age not to put their trust in riches which is so unreliable. Their trust should be in God."

Constant prayer reminds me that when I am content, I can enjoy what God has blessed me with and invest in His kingdom without being controlled by it.

- *Prayer also sets you free from hate and unforgiveness.*

At some point in your life, you came to God and asked for His forgiveness. You admitted your sin, and you asked him to offer you a new chance and a clean slate. It's the beauty and the mystery of God that He forgives.

It's difficult to justify asking God for forgiveness while withholding it from others.

Reread that last line and let it sink in for a minute.

The more you spend time in the word and in prayer with the Father, the more you are changed. You start to see areas of sin in your life that aren't quite right and require repentance. God wants us to offer that same forgiveness to others that He offers to us.

To be sure, it's hard. We aren't God, and we have long memories when it comes to the pain others have caused us. But there's a powerful quote that sums up what happens when we refuse to forgive: "Unforgiveness is like drinking poison and hoping the other person will die."

Praying reminds me of the grace and mercy God showed me and helps me be gracious and merciful to others. If you are struggling with forgiving someone who has hurt you, use your time with God to ask Him to free you from hate and unforgiveness.

- Finally, *prayer guards your heart against temptation and protects us from evil.*

Jesus finishes this model prayer with these words—*and lead us not into temptation but deliver us from the evil one*. Jesus knew a thing or two about the power of temptation. He'd just survived three rounds with the devil. He knew that we would be tested and he wanted us to ask for protection as often as we needed it. We need it daily.

Resisting temptation is not a test of my willpower but of my relationship. When I learn how to spend time cultivating my relationship with Jesus, I become like Jesus. He transforms my heart so I can do what he did—live a pure life. He protects me from the attacks of the evil one and gives me the strength to stand up to the trials.

In 1 Corinthians 10:13, Paul writes, "The temptations in your life are no different from what others experience. And God is faithful. He will not allow the temptation to be more than you can stand. When you are tempted, He will show you a way out so that you can endure."

There's no doubt that there is evil at work in this world. You wouldn't go to battle without armor and a weapon. Jesus reminds us that we have the strength and power of Almighty God at our disposal. All we have to do is ask for His strength. The key to overcoming temptation and trials isn't getting tougher; it's getting closer.

Prayer is connection.

Without it, we are adrift and can only hope to keep our heads above water. With it, we are plugged into the source of life. He is *our* Father. He is holy and exalted. He has a plan for His kingdom, and you are a vital part of that plan. He has a will for you if you'll surrender. He'll take care of your needs today and every day. He forgives our sins and asks us to forgive others. He protects us from temptation and walks with us through trials.

All this is available through prayer.

How strong is your connection?

CHAPTER EIGHTEEN

Be Content

Stop Worrying

D on't borrow trouble. I once heard an elderly lady offer this
advice and it's always stuck with me. And yet, it seems like
most people live frustrated, worry-filled lives. In some cases, we
spend so much time worrying about what *may* happen that it
squeezes everything else out of the way.

Worry, stress, and anxiety are at an all-time high, especially
among young adults.

What's causing this? It's not too hard to find out.

First, we are surrounded by high expectations and the pressure
to succeed. Students regularly face extra testing to ensure they
make the grade. They are enrolled in and busy with traveling sports
leagues to fine-tune their skills. When we reach adulthood we have
the pressure of a career, building a family, saving money, and if we
aren't careful—trying to keep up with the Joneses.

All of this fuels the belief that we can't be happy unless we
have it all.

We're also bombarded with social media. Today's children and teens are constantly connected. It's not surprising that their self-esteem and worldview becomes dependent upon likes, favorites, and comments on their social media posts. But it's not limited to just kids. Adults too are constantly connected—virtually, at least. Both young people and adults substitute virtual relationships for real ones and wonder why they don't have vital connections.

Then there's a world that, let's face it, feels scary and threatening. Between school shootings, global warming doomsday predictions, terrorist attacks, and COVID-19, the news media sells fear, and we are buying. The world suddenly seems very scary indeed.

It's no surprise that we are worry-filled and coming apart at the seams.

The good news is Jesus isn't surprised by worry. He knew this day would come, so he finished this section of the Sermon on the Mount with three keys for a worry-free life.

If you've ever dealt with worry, you know it can come in waves. You think of something that makes you anxious, and it's like a wave peaking and then crashing over you. As soon as that one recedes and you pop to the surface to gasp for breath, you think of something else, and it crashes over you. Then another. And another. Before long, you are drowning in worry and can't keep your head above water.

It's important to note Jesus's use of repetition in Matthew 6:25-34.

Like a lifeguard throwing a ring to a drowning person, three times Jesus says, *therefore...don't worry.* He knew those waves would keep coming at you, and he wanted you to know that each time his promise would be there to pull you through.

So what are the three keys?

First, we must love God above all else.

In case you haven't been paying attention, that's the message of this entire book. When we love God and love others, things tend to take care of themselves. When we love things more than God, we run into problems.

When you are studying the Bible and see the word *therefore*, it's important to consider what that, therefore, is there for. (See what I did there?) A therefore in the Bible means that what immediately comes before is important. In this case, it's the message of Matthew 6:24—*you cannot serve two masters*; if you try, one is always going to get the short end of the stick.

The implication here is that we should be *loving and serving God* first—not money, not stuff.

Many of our worries revolve around provision. Do I have enough money (stuff) to live the life I want to live? When we worry about that, we take our eyes off God. There's a direct relationship between the two. When we love God, commit to serve Him, and keep Him as our focus, our worry diminishes.

Tina and I have a great marriage now, but like every worthwhile journey, the road hasn't always been smooth. Over the years, when we've gone through something difficult or painful, we've learned to say, "Well, at least we have each other!" This mantra has kept us grounded and kept our eyes focused on the right place— strengthening our relationship and doing life together. The point is this—our love brings me so much life, it makes me happy and causes me to feel so secure that *everything else is optional*.

If we lost everything but still had each other, *that* would be enough.

This is how New Testament Christians viewed their relationship with Jesus. The early church was under constant attack, tortured and abused, and lived in a way that today we would consider unbearable and inhumane.

Did they like it? Probably not.

Did it matter? Ultimately, no.

Because Jesus was enough!

Beaten, flogged, shipwrecked, cast out, imprisoned, and ultimately martyred, Paul put it this way in Philippians 3:7-11:

I once thought these things [accomplishments] were valuable, but now I consider them worthless because of what Christ has done. Yes, everything else is worthless when compared with the infinite value of knowing Christ Jesus my Lord. For his sake, I have discarded everything else, counting it all as garbage, so that I could gain Christ and become one with him.

Paul had every reason to love himself and to put himself first. By the standards of the day, he was impressive. He could have been anything and done anything and would have been a success. But in light of Jesus, all of that was garbage and not worth considering. He loved God so much that there was no room for worry, no matter what his circumstances.

It's as simple as this: as our love for Jesus increases, our dependence on the things of this world decreases. Which means that one of life's biggest questions is this: *Is there anything you want more than Jesus?* If so, it will produce worry in your life and crowd out what ultimately brings you peace. When you love Jesus first, it's transformational and it helps us remember the words of Psalm 34:10, "Those who trust in the Lord, lack no good thing." When we love God first, we can trust in Him to provide for our needs—it's the first step in eliminating worry.

Next, we must receive God's love with our whole heart.

Jesus was a great teacher, and he did something interesting here. He tells the crowd not to worry about their lives, food or drink, their health, or even what to wear. I'm sure inwardly some of them groaned. It would be like me telling you the same thing when you don't know where your next meal is coming from or where you are going to sleep tonight. *Oh sure, no problem; I won't worry. Why didn't I think of that?*

Jesus isn't done. At the end of the command not to worry he says, "Isn't life more than food, and your body more than clothing?" He knew we are driven by our appetites, but life is more than that.

Then Jesus, the master of subtleties, looks up at the birds flying in the sky.

In Matthew 6:25-30 he says:

Look at the birds. They don't plant or harvest or store food in barns, for your heavenly Father feeds them. And aren't you far more valuable to Him than they are? Can all your worries add a single moment to your life? And why worry about your clothing? Look at the lilies of the field and how they grow. They don't work or make their clothing, yet Solomon in all his glory was not dressed as beautifully as they are. And if God cares so wonderfully for wildflowers that are here today and thrown into the fire tomorrow, He will certainly care for you. Why do you have so little faith?

I love the phrase *God cares so wonderfully*. God doesn't love you out of obligation. He doesn't love you out of frustration. He loves you *wonderfully*. That means He wants to lavish His love on you and provide you with everything you need for *life*.

Worry stops Him from doing that. Worry is a love-blocker and trust destroyer.

By looking up at the birds and down at the flowers Jesus was demonstrating God's all-encompassing goodness. The world is filled with beauty and wonder that reflects God's goodness, but you and I *were made in God's very image.*

If He cares enough to take care of the birds and clothe flowers in splendor, how much more will He care for us? You have a soul that will live on for eternity. This makes you more valuable than flowers that live, bloom, and die.

Like everyone else, I have a list of things I can choose to worry about. I can worry about my kids and how I am going to afford to get them through college. I can worry about this book I am working on, if I can finish it and how it will be received. I can worry about my friend's marriage that is falling apart. I can worry about the struggling economy, COVID-19, and anything else my brain can throw at me.

There is plenty in this world to worry about, but if God truly loves me, which Jesus assures me He does, then I can trust God will do what is right. I can be assured that He will help me understand my role in His story.

To be fair, choosing to trust God is a choice you must make every day, because worry will find a way to creep back in and blind you to God's love. In Matthew 11:28-30, Jesus gives us one of the most refreshing promises in the Bible: "Come to me, all of you who are weary and carry heavy burdens, and I will give you rest. Take my yoke upon you. Let me teach you, because I am humble and gentle at heart, and you will find rest for your souls. For my yoke is easy to bear, and the burden I give you is light."

We are invited to receive God's love and rest as we work, but it requires giving up control.

At its core, worry revolves around control. We are an extremely self-sufficient, pull yourself up by your bootstraps kind of society. We believe that if we work hard enough (or worry diligently enough), we can take charge of a situation. But like a dog straining at a leash, working under our own power only wears us out and robs us of peace.

It comes back to trusting in God's love. Do you trust Him or yourself more?

If you trust Him, then your circumstances won't derail your faith.

Some people foolishly believe that God is holding out on them. He hasn't given them what *they* want or they lack something they think would make their life better, so they get mad at God. When we rest in God's love, we can trust that He has our best interests in mind. He sees things we don't see. He is more interested in refining our character than making us comfortable.

When we receive God's love with our whole hearts, it has a tendency to elevate our gaze and redirect our focus.

And that leads to the final point—this world is not our home.

We worry because we see all this world has to offer and we think we want it.

But Jesus once again flips the script. In Matthew 6:33, he says, "Seek the Kingdom of God above all else, and live righteously, and He will give you everything you need." We worry when we focus our eyes on the wrong prize. Striving for what this world has to offer is like trying to keep an ice cube in your hand and wondering why it keeps melting. It's temporary. Everything you have, everything you work for may make your life comfortable, but it won't last.

Jesus said to seek what is permanent each day, and you won't have time to worry.

There's a wonderful illustration that Pastor and author Frances Chan did one time in a sermon. You can look it up on YouTube, but here are the basics. Imagine stretching out a hundred-foot long white rope in a straight line. This rope represents eternity. At the one end of the rope is a little piece of red tape, about three-quarters of an inch wide, that wraps around the rope. This little red part represents your life from birth to death.

Get the picture in your mind. The entire rest of the rope represents all the rest of eternity.

When we stress and worry about our life—the red part—we are focused on a tiny small moment of time rather than eternity. Life is hard. I get that, but this world is not our home; this life is temporary. Heaven is our home, and it will last for eternity.

That should be the bulk of our focus and direct how we live our lives each day.

Jesus finishes by saying, "So don't worry about tomorrow, for tomorrow will bring its own worries. Today's trouble is enough for today." When you focus on today and do things that matter for eternity—love others, be kind, share the good news of Christ, worship God, seek peace—you'll find that you squeeze out those worries that used to consume you.

Don't borrow trouble when peace is there for the taking.

CHAPTER NINETEEN

Be Careful

Don't Be Critical

A re you ready to read the most quoted and yet most misunderstood verse in the Bible? Here it is—*Do not judge, or you too will be judged.* Want to talk about a thorny topic? Judgment gets the prize.

In 2007, Barna did an extensive research project in which they asked non-Christian people why they rejected Christianity. Guess what two of the top three reasons were?

87 percent responded that *the church is judgmental.*

85 percent responded that *the church is hypocritical.*

Ouch.

That was not true of Jesus, and if we are going to do what Jesus did, we need to remember the characteristics of Jesus. First, judgment is condemning while Jesus is gracious! I do not know how many times I have heard someone say, "Don't judge me," or, "I'm not one to judge."

Jesus is not saying that we cannot or should not look at someone's life and see their issues. In verses 3-5, Jesus plainly says take care of your own issues first (the log in your eye) before you try to help people with their issues (the speck in their eye). Clearly, we can see each other's faults and have a responsibility to help.

What Jesus is saying is this: Do not write people off as a hopeless cause; do not give up on people, and never assume someone is beyond hope.

The Pharisees and Sadducees looked down their noses at everyone. When people were around them, they felt condemned and hopeless. People could feel their judgment and condemnation. This pushed people away from God.

Jesus looked at everyone—no matter how sin-filled and broken—as worthy of grace.

In Luke chapter 5, Jesus walks by a tax collector's booth and sees Levi. In those days, tax collectors were despised. They were considered traitors for teaming up with the Romans to collect taxes from the Jews. They were not even allowed in the Temple. However, when Jesus sees Levi, he reaches out and makes him a friend.

Levi becomes a follower of Christ and ends up writing a book of the Bible!

Consider the woman caught in adultery in John 8. The religious people hustle her into the street, rocks in hand, ready to stone her to death. Jesus squats to the ground, begins writing what most assume were the 10 Commandments, asks people to consider their own sin, and waits as one by one the stones hit the ground.

In God's mind, failure is not fatal! It's a chance to change direction.

Again and again, we see Jesus reaching out to imperfect people, not in judgment, but in grace. Zacchaeus left the tree and invited Jesus to his house. Peter promised his love three times. Paul was blinded and then saw the light. The woman at the well received the truth and told others. Jesus gave grace to the demon-possessed, to Roman officers, and to Mary Magdalene.

It is a big list of imperfect people.

This should both humble and encourage us—Jesus gives us an example to follow.

I was recently counseling a pastor friend. He sinned; he blew it and is facing the consequences. But here's the deal—he is still my friend. I still love him, and because I love him, I am helping him get the help he needs. This is grace in action.

In Galatians 6:1-2, Paul writes, "Dear brothers and sisters, if another believer is overcome by some sin, you who are godly should gently and humbly help that person back onto the right path. And be careful not to fall into the same temptation yourself. Share each other's burdens, and in this way obey the law of Christ."

Do not judge, or you too will be judged doesn't mean we aren't to recognize when people make mistakes. Rather, we are to offer grace and help them get back on the path. Think about it this way. Have you ever gone hiking in the woods on an established trail? As long as you stay on the path, the way may be bumpy, but the people who have gone before have compacted the dirt; they've cleared away the branches; they've put rocks over the stream, and made it easier for you to reach the end of the trail.

What if you and I are hiking together, but you are walking through the woods about twenty feet off the trail? While I'm strolling along my path, you are blazing a new path over dead limbs and fallen leaves. You have to weave around trees and duck to go under low hanging limbs. You are stumbling over rocks and tripping on obstacles.

If I call out to you and point out that there's an easier way about twenty feet to your left, does that make me judgmental or a friend?

Grace offers a better way. I could let you stumble your way forward, or I could help you out.

That's the difference.

If you spend your life looking down your nose, criticizing, and attacking people who are hurting or suffering, you better hope they never see your imperfection, because if they do, you will be judged; you will be attacked. However, the opposite is true. If you love and help people in their imperfection, then they will help you when you make mistakes.

One of those is drastically better than the other.

- *Judgment is hypocritical, but Jesus is authentic.*

Jesus asks the question, "Why are you worried about the speck in your friend's eye when you have a log in your own eye?" It's kind of humorous. Try to picture a person with a log sticking out of their eye attempting to get close enough to you in order to carefully remove the speck from your eye.

Every time he leans in, *Bam!*, he hits you again with the log hanging out of his eye.

That is what hypocrisy looks like and why everyone hates it. When you pretend you have it all together (ignore the log in your eye), and then try to "help" your brother or sister with the speck in their eye, is it any wonder your help isn't well-received? It is actually painful. Everyone hates hypocrisy. Hypocrisy is ignoring your log, attempting to help everyone else with their speck, while hurting them with your log!

Jesus did not have to worry about hypocrisy because he was perfect. The problem is we aren't. We are not perfect, so how do we overcome our hypocrisy?

Be authentic.

Authenticity is a breath of fresh air. It's admitting you don't have it all figured out, that you do make mistakes sometimes, and that you are working hard to be better and more like Jesus. That's a person anyone can relate to.

People do not expect you to be perfect—especially when you are gracious to other people. The key to avoiding hypocrisy is just refusing to pretend you are perfect. In fact, one of the ways we know the Bible is authentic is it does not attempt to cover the failings of its heroes.

The Bible is transparent and encourages us to be as well.

Another way to understand what Jesus is saying is this: I should spend more time focused on cooperating with God and letting Him change me rather than trying to fix everyone else. Many people spend most of their time pointing out and trying to correct the faults in others while totally ignoring their own issues. I get it. It's much easier for me to try and fix your problems than to work on my own. Unfortunately, that makes me a hypocrite, and you aren't going to listen to me anyway. Then both of us stay broken.

However, when you get the log out of your eye first, then your personal journey of transformation will teach you how to *help other people.* It's time to stop faking it. No one has it all figured out. But when we become authentic together, we can grow and change and become more like Christ.

- ***Judgment is impatient; Jesus is patient.***

Face it, when we judge others for their shortcomings, often it's because we want them to change *now* and get frustrated when they don't. Jesus is incredibly patient. When I look back over my 40-plus years of following Christ, I am so grateful for his patience.

Sometimes, in matters of faith, we try to move people along too fast. Change takes time.

We forget that our job is to be the messenger; God's job is to cause transformation.

When we are pushy with others, we are not pushing them toward Christ but away from him. Jesus advises not to waste what is holy on people who are unholy or not ready. Do not throw your pearls before swine.

Jesus is not being insensitive. We have already seen Jesus cares, and he came to seek and save that which was lost. However, there are times, when we need to recognize that a person's heart is not open yet, and what they need is more love, more friendship, and less preaching.

How do you do that? It's simple. First, build a relationship of trust. Be easy to talk to and quick to listen. Keep confidence and be kind. Then share what Jesus is doing in your life. Be honest but not overbearing. Offer to pray and help with the problems they face in their life. Then look for an open door to share grace and love.

Finally, don't be so easily offended.

Why should we be surprised when lost people swear, drink, and act like the world? If we focus on their behavior before God has a chance to change their heart, we have things out of order and can push people away from Jesus. We write off those Jesus wants us to reach. The truth is, I know some guys who really love Jesus who still cuss occasionally, drink a beer on a hot day, and smoke a cigar.

It is easy to criticize the behavior of others in order to feel better about ourselves when we cannot honestly say we have a close relationship with Jesus, and we are battling secret sin. It is easy to condemn someone else's cussing and justify our gossip. It is easy to condemn someone else's beer and justify our porn. It is easy to condemn someone else's cigar and justify our Big Mac, large fries, and chocolate shake.

Jesus wants us to look inside first and get our own house in order. At the same time, we can love and serve those who don't yet know him with authenticity and patience. Be intentional about connecting with people who do not know Jesus yet and then:

Be gracious. Build people up.

Be authentic. Share your story to give them hope.

Be patient. You share the good news; God transforms.

Persist in pursuing God and let Him take care of the rest.

CHAPTER TWENTY

Be a Follower

Take the Narrow Road

I once heard a story about a couple of guys named Fred and Luke. One day, they were on the side of the road, jumping up and down, frantically waving a hand-crafted sign at every car that was passing by. The sign said, "The End is Near! Turn yourself around now before it's too late!"

One driver that passed didn't appreciate the sign and shouted, "Leave us alone, you religious nuts!" A few seconds later the two men heard the sound of tires screeching followed by a big splash. Fred looked at Luke and said, "Do you think we should just make a sign that says, 'Stop, Bridge Out Ahead'?"

The story may be humorous, but warnings are there for a reason. And as Jesus was finishing up his first sermon, he gave us three important warnings:

- Don't follow the crowd.
- Don't follow false teachers.
- Don't follow your feelings.

- *First, he warned us not to follow the crowd.*

In Jesus's day, there were two types of religion.

The first was Jewish Orthodoxy, which had lost its connection with God and had been reduced to a system of rules and religious ceremony. It was like much of the religion you see in Western culture today. There were lots of rules, lots of rituals, but no relational connection.

The Romans, on the other hand, were polytheistic. They believed in many gods, each one as good as the next. The vast majority of people who stood on the hillside that day had *some* kind of religion, but they were totally disconnected from God.

So as his sermon drew to a close in Matthew 7:13-14, Jesus laid down a challenge—*Don't follow the crowd.* He knew the people wanted to find their own way to heaven; he also knew that simply following the crowd—whether Jewish or Roman—wouldn't get you there.

So he uses a word picture of a narrow gate and a broad road to demonstrate the cost of following him. Most people choose the broad road. It's easy to follow the crowd and to passively give in to the influence of culture. This road is wide, crowded, and noisy because it's filled with lots of other people. Jesus says this is the road most are traveling.

The only problem is that it's an easy-to-follow path that leads to destruction.

The narrow gate is difficult.

Why?

Because it can be a lonely road, a quiet road, a road with ongoing challenges. The narrow road is a road of humble dependence. Following Jesus is an exercise in humility. It forces you to come to grips with your sin and independence. Following Jesus requires you to repent and change direction. Repentance means leaving the wide and popular road and heading down the narrow road less traveled. It means taking your hands off the wheel and letting Jesus take over.

For many, this is difficult to accept. It certainly was for the rich young ruler in Matthew 19:16-30. Listen to his conversation with Jesus:

"Teacher, what good deed must I do to have eternal life?"

This man was trying to find his way to eternal life. He came to the right person and asked the right question but notice what happens next.

"Why do you ask me about what is good?" Jesus replied. "There is only One who is good. If you want to enter life, keep the commandments."

"Which ones?" he inquired.

Jesus replied, "'You shall not murder, you shall not commit adultery, you shall not steal, you shall not give false testimony, honor your father and mother,' and 'love your neighbor as yourself.'"

"All these I have kept," the young man said. "What do I still lack?"

Jesus answered, "If you want to be perfect, go, sell your possessions and give to the poor, and you will have treasure in heaven. Then come, follow me."

When the young man heard this, he went away sad, because he had great wealth.

Then Jesus said to his disciples, "Truly I tell you, it is hard for someone who is rich to enter the kingdom of heaven. Again I tell you, it is easier for a camel to go through the eye of a needle than for someone who is rich to enter the kingdom of God."

When the disciples heard this, they were greatly astonished and asked, "Who then can be saved?" Jesus looked at them and said, "With man this is impossible, but with God all things are possible."

The point of this story isn't about the money. It's about the *decision* the rich young ruler faced about which path to take. One path meant surrender. The other meant self-reliance.

Jesus came looking for followers, not fans.

The rich young ruler would probably have been willing to be a Jesus *fan*. Who wouldn't want a cool friend who does miracles? He could keep his stuff and support Jesus with everything but his heart.

Jesus wanted more. He came to make disciples. Followers.

The issue always boils down to this—are you going to be in charge, or is Jesus going to be in charge? The wide road says you can be in charge of your own life; you don't have to submit to anyone or anything, and there are many ways to be blessed and spend eternity in heaven. In John 14:6, Jesus made it clear there's only one: "*I am the way, the truth, and the life. No one comes to the Father but by me.*"

- *Second, Jesus warned us not to follow false teachers.*

One of the dangers of living in the information age is we are bombarded constantly with false information and conflicting messages. Often it is difficult or even impossible to discern the truth.

Jesus said watch out! Beware of these false teachers and false information. In first-century Judaism, the Sadducees, Pharisees, and Zealots disagreed about theology, the path to spiritual maturity, political and cultural engagement. In the Roman Empire, religion was a means to an end. They worshiped the gods to gain prosperity and blessings for their families and communities. These gods did not have high moral standards. Instead, approval was gained through religious rituals, prayers, and sacrifice.

It was in this context Jesus says beware. Do not follow the crowd down the wrong spiritual path, and watch out for false teachers. So who do we follow? What is the truth? Jesus would say *examine their fruit.*

When you look at the life of Jesus, his character, his lifestyle, and his fruit stand out above all the rest. Generally speaking, you can look at the fruit and learn a lot about the tree. Jesus was rooted in the Father; consequently, he bore good fruit.

When the disciples of John the Baptist were losing hope as he was locked away in prison, they came to ask Jesus, *Are you the one?* They wanted to be sure they weren't giving up everything for a false teacher. In Matthew 11:4-5, Jesus replied, "Go back and report to John what you hear and see: The blind receive sight, the lame walk, those who have leprosy are cleansed, the deaf hear, the dead are raised, and the good news is proclaimed to the poor."

It was his way of saying, look at my fruit.

- ***Third, Jesus warned us to not follow an experience.***

We love to trust our feelings, yet our feelings constantly lead us astray.

It's human nature to trust what we can see and sense, and yet, we must build our theology and our lives on the practice and example of Jesus. In Matthew 7:21-23, Jesus (once again) called out the hypocrites of the day.

The Pharisees were masters at looking religious and pouring out judgment on those who didn't meet their standards of righteousness.

From the outside, their acts of piety made them look close to God, but inside they were rotten.

True followers of Jesus do not simply *act* like Jesus but *become* like Jesus.

Their actions are a reflection of who they are.

Experiences may feel great in the moment. They may look good on social media. But they are a poor substitute for an authentic relationship with Jesus. An authentic relationship produces more than religious customs and rituals. An authentic relationship with Jesus produces transformation. Jesus said if we abide in him, if we have an authentic life-giving connection, we will bear much fruit (John 15:1-5). Paul said the fruit of God's Spirit is love, joy, peace, patience, kindness, goodness, gentleness, faithfulness, and self-control.

In other words, when we are connected to Jesus we become like Jesus and everyone can *see* the fruit in our lives. If you want to live your best life—a truly blessed life—it requires more than being a fan of Jesus. We have to follow Jesus. We have to take the narrow path, build our lives on the teachings of Jesus—*not* our feelings or experiences.

This is the path, the road, the way to a blessed life, and Jesus is leading the way.

Be Unshakeable

Build on the Rock

I grew up on the Atlantic coast, and through the years we experienced several hurricanes. From the safety of our home, we felt the lashing of the high winds, the machine-gun patter of lots of rain hitting the walls, windows, and roof, and saw the spray of big waves pounding the shore.

It was always fascinating to drive down to the beach after the storm had blown through and see what had been washed away. Often there would be a row of houses, standing in the receding water. The yard, trees, and everything else had washed away in the punishing storm, but the house was still standing strong. It was built on a solid foundation.

Life is just like this.

In life, you will experience storms. The question is will your house and your life stand strong in the middle of the storm? The key is building on a strong foundation.

When Jesus closes his message, he ends by talking about building such a house.

It's a metaphor that everyone would have understood, and it still works for us today.

One of the biggest purchases most people will ever buy is their house. Their house provides shelter from the rain, wind, heat, and cold. It's a place to raise a family and welcome community. When you build a house, you want to make sure it has a firm foundation and a strong structure. Otherwise, it could crumble when the storms come.

And the storms will come.

In life, just as in homebuilding, we must be prepared for the storms. Things rarely go as planned, and when the inevitable bumps, bruises, and detours arise, we need to be sure we are built on a solid foundation. This is the only way to ensure your house will stand.

Religion looks great in the sun, but it fails in the storms.

When the storms come, you need more than religion; you need God.

The only way to ensure you are in a right relationship with God is to build on the words Jesus taught and put them into practice in your daily life. In Matthew 7:24-27, Jesus draws a contrast between a wise and a foolish builder. The implication is clear. The wise build their lives on Jesus, the truth, and his teaching. This is the solid rock. The foolish choose a different foundation. This is the shifting sand.

So the question for you is this: what are you building your house on?

If it is anything other than Jesus, the storm will erode your foundation.

Storms expose your foundation. When you have a storm in your marriage, you discover some things about your heart and your relationship. When you have a storm in your body, you discover some things about your health, your eating, your exercise, your weight, or your blood pressure. When you have a storm in your finances, you discover some things about your spending, priorities, and your career.

You can have a storm in any area of your life, and the storm will always expose your foundation. So the question to ask *before* the storm is, *What am I building my marriage, my physical health, or my financial future on?* Jesus is trying to help us to understand if we will build our lives on the foundation of Jesus and his word, our house will stand!

At each point in my life where my foundation was exposed, I was able to make a choice—watch it crumble or build a new foundation. When the storms come, you can despise the storm (this is what most people do) and say, *Why is this happening to me?* Or, you can despise the bad foundation and start digging. We are all works in progress, and in light of that, the storms can actually help you. They can highlight small cracks now that may become catastrophic failures later. Sometimes the storms confirm that you are building upon the rock; other times they reveal you are building on the sand. Either way, the storm can be a benefit if you'll let it.

At the end of his first sermon, Jesus drove home one point—build your life upon me.

That message is echoed throughout the rest of the New Testament.

- Jesus is foundational. "In the beginning, the Word already existed. The Word was with God, and the Word was God. He existed in the beginning with God. God created everything through him, and nothing was created except through him. The Word gave life to everything that was created, and his life brought light to everyone" (John 1:1-4).

- *Jesus is the gatekeeper.* "I am the way, the truth, and the life. No one can come to the Father except through me" (John 14:6).

- *Jesus is the cornerstone.* "You are coming to Christ, who is the living cornerstone of God's temple. He was rejected by people, but he was chosen by God for great honor. And you are living stones that God is building into His spiritual temple" (1 Peter 2:4-6).

- *Jesus is primary.* "Because of God's grace to me, I have laid the foundation like an expert builder. Now others are building on it. But whoever is building on this foundation must be very careful. For no one can lay any foundation other than the one we already have- Jesus Christ" (1 Corinthians 3:10-11).

- *Jesus is bedrock.* "You are the Messiah, the Son of the living God ... upon this rock, I will build my church and all the powers of Hell will not conquer it" (Matthew 16:16, 18).

If you want your life to be unshakeable, you must build your life on Jesus!

One of the most heartbreaking and frustrating parts of being a pastor is seeing, over and over again, people who decide to ignore Jesus and his teaching. They come to church and hear the word a couple of times a month but never put what they hear into practice. When a small storm comes, it all comes crashing down. Often, the crash is so great you cannot repair the damage. Sometimes it is a total loss, and they walk away from the faith.

Sadly, pastors can make the same mistake. In fact, studies have shown that pastors who fall morally have these common characteristics. They lacked personal accountability. They had no one to answer to and no one to share their struggles with. They had no devotional life. The Bible was something they studied to preach but not something they connected to in worship. They believed their foundation was secure and that nothing "would ever happen to me."

They *knew* the truth, but did not *build* on it. They did not obey their own teaching, much less the teaching of Jesus. The secret to your life is not *what you know* but *what you do* with what you know.

These same cracks can develop in your own foundation if you aren't careful.

In fact, the wisest person of all, Solomon, who explains in Proverbs 1:1-7 why wisdom is critical, ignored his own teaching. Consequently, he destroyed his life and put his kingdom in a death spin. His house fell, and he died disgraced.

So how do we avoid a shattered foundation and become like Jesus?

Through humble dependence.

We pride ourselves on our independence, but that is the same thing as building on shifting sand. It is time to expose our foundation of pride and independence so we can do something about it before it's too late. When we do, we change. We are:

- Not a Burden but a Blessing
- Not Outside In but Inside Out
- Not Angry but Peacemakers
- Not Immoral but Moral
- Not Selfish but Selfless

- Not Hypocrites but people of Integrity
- Not Servant but Sons
- Not Hate-filled but Love-driven
- Not Greed-seekers but Generosity-givers
- Not Worry-filled but Faith-trusting
- Not Insecure but Secure

This is the life everyone wants, but it only comes through humble dependence on Jesus.

This list makes us unshakeable in the face of storms.

The wise person builds on the solid rock of Jesus's teaching.

The wise person doesn't fear the storm, but leans into the wind with the power of God.

The wise person listens to the word and then does what it says.

Storms will come. Is your foundation secure?

YOUR LIFE REDEFINED

Y ou've probably heard the story of the Prodigal Son. It's a powerful illustration of the lengths a parent will go to reach their child and a tangible representation of humanity's relationship with God. It's also a wonderful way to wrap up this book.

In Luke 15 Jesus tells the story:

There was a man who had two sons. The younger one said to his father, "Father, give me my share of the estate." So he divided his property between them.

Not long after that, the younger son got together all he had, set off for a distant country, and there squandered his wealth in wild living. After he had spent everything, there was a severe famine in that whole country, and he began to be in need. So he went and hired himself out to a citizen of that country, who sent him to his fields to feed pigs. He longed to fill his stomach with the pods that the pigs were eating, but no one gave him anything.

When he came to his senses, he said, "How many of my father's hired servants have food to spare, and here I am starving to death! I will set out and go back to my father and say to him: Father, I have sinned against heaven and against you. I am no longer worthy to be called your son; make me like one of your hired servants."

So he got up and went to his father. But while he was still a long way off, his father saw him and was filled with compassion for him; he ran to his son, threw his arms around him, and kissed him.

The son said to him, "Father, I have sinned against heaven and against you. I am no longer worthy to be called your son." But the father said to his servants, "Quick! Bring the best robe and put it on him. Put a ring on his finger and sandals on his feet. Bring the fattened calf and kill it. Let's have a feast and celebrate. For this son of mine was dead and is alive again; he was lost and is found."

So they began to celebrate.

Meanwhile, the older son was in the field. When he came near the house, he heard music and dancing. So he called one of the servants and asked him what was going on. "Your brother has come," he replied, "and your father has killed the fattened calf because he has him back safe and sound."

The older brother became angry and refused to go in. So his father went out and pleaded with him. But he answered his father, "Look! All these years I've been slaving for you and never disobeyed your orders. Yet you never gave me even a young goat so I could celebrate with my friends. But when this son of yours who has squandered your property with prostitutes comes home, you kill the fattened calf for him!"

"My son," the father said, "you are always with me, and everything I have is yours. But we had to celebrate and be glad, because this brother of yours was dead and is alive again; he was lost and is found."

When you read this story, which son are you?

Are you the son who dishonored his father (God), lived in immorality, but finally humbled himself, returning to the father in brokenness, surrender, and dependence?

Or are you the other son who has been "slaving away, all these years" when there is blessing just around the corner? Here is what we need to understand about these two sons.

First, both of these sons were far from their father. The prodigal left town, blew his inheritance, and destroyed his life. We can all see his sin. We can all see how desperately he needs his father.

On the other hand, the older son still lives at home. He has been slaving away, doing what he thinks is expected, and desperately trying to *earn* his father's love. Despite years of hard work (what we would call religion), his heart is far from the father.

He is tired, angry, prideful, judgmental, frustrated, alone, discouraged, and confused.

Maybe you have felt that way.

Second, the father loved both sons, and he demonstrated that by his actions. Each day, the father left the house and went looking for both sons. It's easy to imagine the father stepping outside each evening to look for the older son returning from the fields while hoping to see the younger son returning from his folly.

Here's the lesson for us—it does not matter which son you are. What does matter is God loves you and is searching for you! God is desperate to have a relationship with you. In fact, Jesus tells this story to explain to the religious leaders in his day *why* he spends so much time with sinners rather than hiding in the church.

Jesus came to seek and save that which is lost.

Whether you are lost in religion or immorality, the Father is searching for you.

Here's the last and best part of the story—God is ready to celebrate your return. The prodigal son has hit rock bottom. He looks around at his surroundings and admits something many of us have felt: *I never expected to end up here.*

Maybe that is how you feel now.

Maybe you are looking around at your life and thinking, I never *intended* to end up here.

In a moment of clarity, the prodigal son realizes if he were a slave in his father's house, he would be better off than the life he's living now, so he heads home. The prodigal sees his father standing on the hillside, and with a lump in his throat he says the words that he's been practicing all the way home, "I am not worthy to be a son."

Although it took courage to admit that, the truth is neither son is worthy. In fact, nothing we will ever do makes us worthy of the Father's love. Ultimately, that doesn't matter because God's love is not based on *what we do* but *who He is.*

The son expects to be rejected and punished by his father. I think many people feel this way about God. I once had a lady who was visiting our church for the first time tell me that she was afraid God would kill her if she ever stepped foot in church. That is how the prodigal son must have felt as he walked toward the father he had rejected.

But rather than judgment, anger, or wrath, what the son experienced was love, mercy, and grace. In fact, far from being disappointed, the father throws a party to celebrate the son's return! Jesus says, in verse 7 of this same chapter, "I tell you that in the same way there will be more rejoicing in heaven over one sinner who repents than over ninety-nine righteous persons who do not need to repent."

This message should seep into your soul today. Whether you are in the far country living your own way or slaving away in religion, if you will return to the father, He is ready to celebrate your return.

How do you find your way home? Just like the prodigal, we approach the father with:

- **Humility**—*Jesus, I am bankrupt without you.*

- **Brokenness**—*Jesus, I am sorry for the mess I have created and the pain I have caused.*

- **Surrender**—*Jesus, I am done with being in charge, I am ready to follow.*

- **Dependence**—*Jesus, I cannot do this without you.*

This is the way home. When we return to the father from the far country or from slaving away in the field of religion, something amazing happens. We start to look more and more like our Father.

I have a visible reminder of this in my own life. Today, my dad and I have reconciled and are good friends. One of our favorite things to do is play golf together. On my refrigerator, I have a golf picture. It was taken at a charity tournament and made into a refrigerator magnet. When I look at that picture each day, I am amazed by how much I look like my dad.

When we come home to the Father and learn to live in His presence, we grow up to "look like our Dad." We are merciful to those in the far country and those still slaving away in religion. We are authentic. We no longer live to please people but to please our Father. We are peacemakers. We are more concerned about people than being right.

We live by faith.

In the midst of our suffering, we know who our Father is and what our future holds.

Now, as sons and daughters of God, we are led by *love*, not *laws*. We are the salt and light of the world. God is producing His life in us, and we are sharing that life with our world. This is the Christian life. Jesus came to reunite us with the Father so we could live in His love.

Are you ready to come home? Start with this prayer:

"Jesus, I humble myself before you. I have sinned against you. I am not worthy of your love. I am sorry for the mess I have made and the pain I have caused. I am no longer in charge. I am ready to follow. I cannot do this without you. Today, I receive your love, mercy, and grace. I am trusting you to produce your life in me. I am your son/daughter. Help me to live in love. Whatever you want me to do, whatever you want me to be, wherever you want me to go, my life is yours."

This is what Jesus came to do. It's where your life begins.

This is religion *redefined*.

ABOUT THE AUTHOR

F ailure isn't fatal. God can redeem your biggest failure, your worst tragedy, and your darkest sin. If you open your heart to Jesus and are willing to take the journey, the best is yet to be!

As a sophomore in college, Allen realized God was calling him into full-time ministry. After graduating from UNCW in 1996, Allen moved to Wake Forest, NC to begin seminary at Southeastern Baptist Theological Seminary. Shortly thereafter, Allen married Tina. However, after five months of marriage, they found themselves in the middle of a marriage crisis.

Like many people, Allen was a decent person who loved Jesus. However, internally he was insecure, driven, and striving–desperately trying to earn God's approval and the approval of those around him. God began to transform Allen's life from the inside out and heal his pain and brokenness. During this season, Allen learned how to live in the presence of God, which transformed everything.

In 1998, Pastor Allen returned to seminary and finished his Master of Divinity. In October of 2000, Allen and Tina moved to Greensboro, NC to begin pastoring Definition Church. For the last 20 years, Pastor Allen and Tina have openly shared their redemption story and inspired thousands to enter into a life-changing relationship with Jesus. Meanwhile, Definition Church has grown from 35 to several thousand.

Pastor Allen then attended Gordon-Conwell where he earned his Doctorate of Ministry degree in Redemptive Leadership. God has used his story and his message to produce hope and a redemptive path for all who are willing to take the journey with Christ.

Today Allen and Tina have been married for 24 years and have an incredible marriage and three incredible children, Luke, Abigail, and Isabella. In addition to doing anything with Tina and the family, Pastor Allen enjoys hunting, golf, writing or reading a great book.